THE COMMUNITY OF THE FUTURE

by Arthur E. Morgan:

SEARCH FOR PURPOSE

NOWHERE WAS SOMEWHERE

THE SMALL COMMUNITY

INDUSTRIES FOR SMALL COMMUNITIES

A BUSINESS OF MY OWN

THE RURAL UNIVERSITY

THE MIAMI CONSERVANCY DISTRICT

EDWARD BELLAMY: A BIOGRAPHY

THE PHILOSOPHY OF EDWARD BELLAMY

MY WORLD

PURPOSE AND CIRCUMSTANCE

A COMPENDIUM OF ANTIOCH NOTES

THE SEED MAN

THE LONG ROAD

THE COMMUNITY
OF THE FUTURE

AND

The Future of Community

by ARTHUR E. MORGAN

President, Community Service, Inc.

Former Chairman, Tennessee Valley Authority

Former President, Antioch College

COMMUNITY SERVICE, INCORPORATED
YELLOW SPRINGS, OHIO

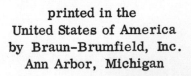

printed in the
United States of America
by Braun-Brumfield, Inc.
Ann Arbor, Michigan

CONTENTS

PART ONE

I. Introduction

There is a feeling toward human affairs, especially in America, that what is small or local is unimportant. We see bigness as a measure of significance. From this point of view the community, being small, can be of little consequence. It deals with the common affairs of life, with the detailed and the particular.

Yet it is details and particulars which inform us most directly of the nature and the realities of life. Hallam Tennyson wrote in his story of Vinoba Bhave, "The universal is profoundly different from the cosmopolitan"; and "Simeon Stylites," columnist for *The Christian Century*, expressed the same idea:[1]

> Only the local is universal. Literature in all countries attests it. The concrete, specific, local thing has a survival value far surpassing that of the abstract in general. As Oliver Wendell Holmes put it, "Identification with a locality is a surer passport to immortality than cosmopolitanism." The local is the only thing of interest in all the nooks and corners of the map and the calendar. In fact, the only thing of no universal interest is the universe. A friend of Goethe's, Johann Heinrich Merck, wrote: "Everything for the ancients was local, for the moment, and that is why it became eternal."

Yet the local and the particular are of great interest only as they are representative of something much more than themselves. A man does not know himself until he has discovered that what seems particular in himself is part of the universal. As Emerson said: "To believe your own thought, to believe that what is true for you in your private heart is true for all men, —that is genius. Speak your latest conviction, and it shall be the universal sense." The community is important because it has in it that of the particular which is eternal and universal. It is for that reason that when a culture severs

contact with community it must somehow renew that relationship if its full life is to continue.

This discussion deals with the future of the community,
and with *The Community of the Future*. During the past fifteen years the literature concerning community has multiplied
to perhaps ten times what it had been. It is doubtful whether
light on the subject has increased proportionally. A large
number of detailed research projects, not all of them inspired,
have somewhat broadened the basis for thinking in the field,
and the many accounts of community betterment projects at
best illustrate how good ideas may be put into practice.

For the past fifty years there has been a class of writing
which fervently treated the small rural community as a holy
cause. Much of this has been nostalgic, rather than critical. It
could almost be summed up by the slogan, "Back to the farm."

We confess to zeal in our own writing in this general field.
It has been our effort to be responsible and representative in
statements made, while arousing concern for the fate of community in our rapidly changing society. We hope for a continuing, critically discriminating interest and energy in presenting
this issue, which we believe to be vital to human well-being,
and which has had very inadequate consideration. In this present writing we have endeavored more specifically to point out
the inherent limitations and disadvantages of typical small
communities as they have existed up to the present, as well
as their vital significance; and to indicate what elements of
urban life are of such sure value that they should be included
in an enduring cultural inheritance.

The past gives us our sole basis for thinking about the future. To think effectively of the possible future of the small
community we must know something of its history; of its past
character and significance. We should not be justified in assuming that the general reader, or even the general sociologist, is sufficiently well informed on that subject for us to
pass it by.

In general, recognition of the small, face-to-face community as a vital, and to a large degree controlling, factor in
human life, is only just beginning to be current. The clear
concept is less than a hundred years old. Such fundamental

ideas diffuse slowly. For instance, the Copernican theory, that the earth is not the center of creation, but is a planet moving about the sun, was more than a century old before it was accepted, even by most of the leading scientific minds.

It is a half-century or more since a few men began to recognize the historic part the village community has played in human affairs. Henry Sumner Maine described the ancient village as it once had been in England and as he found it still surviving in India. Frederic Le Play of France, after his widespread studies in western Europe, central Asia and Scandinavia, described its characteristics with clarity and penetration. Ferdinand Tönnies did somewhat the same for the Germanic countries, and Charles H. Cooley in America contributed his great insight to an understanding of the nature and significance of community. Somewhat later Dwight Sanderson of Cornell, in *The Rural Community,* assembled valuable data concerning rural cultures the world over. During the past 25 years a number of rural sociologists have produced well-written textbooks in the field.

Except for the persons first mentioned, most writers up to the past 10 or 15 years looked at the small community as a phase of agricultural society, though it had long antedated agriculture, and never was limited to it. One well-known sociologist expressed the prevailing view: "Rural sociology is the sociology of the agricultural calling"; while a president of the Rural Sociological Society wrote: "Rural non-farm, one of the United States Census categories, is almost a contradiction in terms." Yet already the "rural non-farm" is greater than the farm population.

Since the establishment of Community Service, Inc., about 15 years ago, we have contended that the face-to-face community is a fundamental and necessary unit of society; that, along with the family, it has been and continues to be the chief medium for transmitting the basic cultural inheritance; and that if such is the case it is far too important to rest on any single calling, such as agriculture. Because the part which it has played and probably must continue to play in our common life has been much overlooked, we have persistently drawn attention to its importance.

Much of what is written about the theory of community is constantly clouded and cumbered by the doctrinaire, and especially by the attitude of either-or. For instance, some of our sociological friends state that the issue is between the formal and the informal structure of society; that we can have one, but not both, and must take our choice. "Gemeinschaft," made familiar by the writing of the German sociologist, Tönnies, is a name for informal, spontaneous social groups, not the result of formal, deliberate organization. A neighborhood group, or an informal frequent getting together by bankers to agree on policies, or the informal group which met with Socrates, would be cases of gemeinschaft. "Gesellschaft" is a name for formal organization, such as a legally incorporated business, or a state with a written constitution, or a deliberately organized boy-scout troop. The community is an informal—gemeinschaft—institution. Some of our prominent sociological friends hold that the way of the world is toward formal, gesellschaft, organization, that therefore the day of the small community is past, and that it may as well be forgotten.

This seems to us almost like saying that we must make our choice between positive and negative electricity, that we cannot have both. Informal, spontaneous organization constantly tends to take on formal structure, while formal organization is a dead shell unless it is vitalized by informal, spontaneous group life. Formal government usually is given character and direction by spontaneous group action, often behind the scenes. The high school student studies about the formal, gesellschaft, organization of government; the political boss or leader shares in an informal, gemeinschaft, group which influences government. The church congregation has its constitution and rules and authority, its formal structure, but unless an informal spirit of brotherhood and commitment gives it life, it is but a hollow shell or an instrument of power. The informal spirit of community is the vital social spirit that inhabits and gives life to the formal organizations of society.

Another of the "either-or" dicta of some professional sociologists and political theorists is that we must decide between the supremacy of the individual and the supremacy of the social group. In Russia, we are told, the state is supreme, and the individual counts only as its means or instrument. In America, we are informed, except as our social structure has been recently contaminated by subversive ideas, the individual is supreme, and the function of the state is only as a keeper of order. The idea of the community, these theorists hold, is obsolescent because it assumes that the community has personality and life of its own, which has continuing existence and character.

Here, again, the either-or dogma is false. In fact the individual has his own separate existence and personality which it is the responsibility of society to recognize; but also the community has its existence, spirit and character, to which the individual contributes. As an extreme example, the Eskimos of the Coronation Gulf region have individual separateness much exceeding our own; yet their communities, as communities, except as disrupted by "civilization," are living social organisms with very marked character and personality. (Incidentally, Eskimos have substantially larger brains than we of European stock. Perhaps that is why they can hold in a single synthesis elements that many people consider to be mutually exclusive!)

A person reading this book will easily observe some of its limitations. It is not the work of a scholar. There are few citations or quotations, and most of those few are from outside the field of sociological literature. There is no over-all orderly treatment of the subject. Rather there are comments on various matters relating to community. If there is continuity it is of spirit and attitude, rather than of the treatment of subject matter. This is not a matter of choice, but of necessity. When a person, approaching his eightieth year, while deterred by incessant interruptions is trying to make a record of some of his thoughts, time steps on his heels and bids him not delay, or be too much concerned with orderly presentation. This is all the more the case when orderly presentation never was a strong point.

Nor is there an orderly setting forth of data, reasoning and conclusion. That fact does not trouble me much. Quite generally the appearance of orderly development is misleading. What is commonly presented in serious writing is a series of intuitions tied together by a seeming thread of logic. Sometimes we should get more out of such expressions if the seeming logic were omitted, and if the substance were presented for what it is—an assemblage of somewhat related ideas. Sometimes, as in the case of Ralph Waldo Emerson, this process goes so far that what results is little more than a series of aphorisms, not much more closely tied together than those in the Biblical book of Proverbs, or in Shakespeare's plays.

Notwithstanding this lack of structure there is a certain thread of unity, of aim, though expressed in a variety of moods. The burden of that message is that in the nearly universal basic core of the cultural tradition of mankind there are values which are essential to the continuity and health of human society. Some conditions of living are more favorable than others to the preservation of those essential elements. If we depart too far from the conditions of living which favor the preservation and vigor of those elements, the effect on the whole of society may be disastrous. Present-day society is tending, by its very physical organization and structure, to depart from those favorable conditions, with adverse results which are becoming evident, but the reasons for which are not generally recognized.

This priceless treasure of the cultural tradition is interwoven with other elements which are obsolescent or mistaken and which are definitely harmful, or cumbersome impediments to society. The problem is to disentangle and to remove the undesirable elements and to strengthen and supplement those which are vital to well-being. This process can have the assistance of critical inquiry and appraisal. Neither the cultural inheritance nor the process of critical appraisal and of creative thinking is infallible, and the working out of the program of living calls for practical skill, judgment and experience.

To some degree the small, face-to-face community seems the most promising setting in which to work out this issue and to carry on a desirable way of living. In other respects urban life and the contributions it has made are fundamental. It remains to develop a new synthesis of social form, custom and spirit which will combine the available values from all sources, and avoid the negative elements we now contend with.

Such is the theme. Yet the development of technology and the flux of common life are bringing about such great changes in living that the function of the community needs to be re-examined. What, if anything, is its significance today? What place, if any, will it have in the society of the future? The "if any" is important. We should repeatedly examine the assumption that the community has great value for today, and especially for the strange, new days to come. May we be simply carrying over past or present ideas into new circumstances for which they are inapplicable? Are there what we may call community qualities which are so vital to survival and welfare under any possible social circumstances—just as men will continue to need to breathe air and to drink water, regardless of social change—that we do well to plan for their survival and nurture regardless of what forms of society may emerge from unprecedented technical revolution and social transformation? If so, can we identify those qualities, and can we be reasonably sure as to what elements of physical and social environment will favor their development?

Are there characteristically urban values which are similarly important, and which must be woven into the texture of any enduringly good society? Why has there been flight from the village to the city in all parts of the world? What qualities does urban life have which appeal so generally? Is it possible to unite the values of both types of society and to avoid the evils and shortcomings of both? Can there be a community of the future which will save what has been so vital to men in the village life of the past, and at the same time capture those desirable qualities of urban life which through the centuries have had wholesome and legitimate appeal? What should be the characteristics of that community of the future, and what can we do to bring them into being? These are the issues to which we address ourselves.

II

What We Mean by Community

Before discussing the community of the future it may be well to make clear what we mean by "community." The word is used in two senses: as a quality of society, and as the name of a particular kind of local population group.

First, as a quality of life. In thinking of our physical bodies we take for granted such organs as eyes or lungs without thinking of the hundreds of millions of years which went into their evolution. So in thinking of human society we seldom give thought to the slow evolution of the cultural inheritance which is its essence, and without which it could not exist.

We somewhat confusedly recognize the difference between, on the one hand, inborn biological characteristics such as eyes and lungs and inborn traits such as hunger, fear and the sex impulse, and on the other hand the socially determined characteristics of society. The biological traits, including inborn instincts or other inborn drives, are transmitted from generation to generation in the process of physical reproduction. Our distinctly social traits, such as mutual trust and confidence and loyalty to general principles, may have had some faint beginnings as inborn traits, but in their present condition they are not born in us as are the inclination to hunger or the sex drive; rather, they are acquired by learning after we are born. They are continued from generation to generation by the contagion of example—by living and participating in a society where those traits are present. By and large, if a person grows up in a society where such socially determined traits are not present in his associates, he will not acquire them himself.

Human speech, including the variety we call English, probably began with our prehuman ancestors as simple cries, growls and grunts, some of them as expressions of inborn impulse, and much like the vocal sounds of other animals.

Doubtless a very long period elapsed during the slow, gradual evolution of such voice sounds into what we recognize as human speech. An infant cries at birth from inborn impulse. At maturity, as a result of his cultural inheritance, he speaks his mother tongue. There is no sudden break between the infant cry and the mature speech; yet they are fundamentally different in that one takes its character from inborn impulse and the other from the society in which one lives. The cry of the child at birth is the same in all races and cultures. The speech of men varies according to the cultural inheritance. So, various of our other cultural traditions doubtless began in small, rudimentary expressions, perhaps from inborn traits, and slowly accumulated content, quality and variety. This process of cultural evolution could take place only in the small social groups—villages—in which nearly all of humanity has lived throughout the long ages until very recent times.

It has taken many hundreds of thousands of years for these social traits to develop from small and varied beginnings and to become stabilized. We realize that in biological evolution if there is failure for a single generation to have offspring, that line will be extinct. If, for any reason whatever, there are no children, there will be no grandchildren. We sometimes fail to recognize that the same holds true as to our social inheritance. If a person has no chance to experience good will, considerateness, courtesy, and mutual helpfulness in the life around him, then in general he will not have those qualities in himself. Some persons learn such socially acquired traits more readily than others, just as some children learn to speak the mother tongue more readily and more accurately than others; but just as even the most intelligent person, if he had not heard English spoken would not be able to speak it, so if a person has not been exposed to these qualities he will not come to possess them.

These traits of mutuality which men get by living together in intimate relationships—which include intimate acquaintance, mutual confidence, regard, and responsibility, a sharing of the risks and opportunities of life, and a feeling of oneness—turn a group of individuals into a social organism. They have not only individual characters and minds, but a group character and a group mind. It is this interwoven and interrelated complex of social traits, this social personality, which we have in mind when we speak of community as a quality of society.

The effect of community on the individuals concerned varies greatly in different societies. Among the Hutterites— compact religious communities which originated in the regions bordering on Switzerland, then spent a couple of centuries as refugees in Russia, and are now located in South Dakota and nearby states and Manitoba—community tends to infringe on individual personality. As an elder in one Hutterite community put it, "A boy's spirit must be broken by the time he is thirteen." As already mentioned, among the Eskimos around Coronation Gulf, north of Canada, the exact opposite condition prevails. While among them there is a very high degree of mutual regard and responsibility, there is also very strong adherence to individuality. One way of respecting that personal autonomy is by refraining from bringing pressure on any member. This considerateness goes so far that if part of the village is going on a hunting trip and another part is going fishing, it would be considered very improper for even husband or wife to try to persuade the other. If he wants to go with the hunters and she with the fishing party, neither must try to influence the other as to which to do. Mass living may be tyrannously regimented, and very close community may preserve individuality unimpaired, or the contrary may be true in each case.

Human society cannot exist without some degree of this quality of community. Even a gang of cutthroats cannot continue as a gang unless there is some degree of confidence among the members that they will not practice their throat-cutting on each other. Without some degree of such confidence the gang would fall apart and each person would look out for himself. It is because mutual confidence—the spirit of community—is inadequate among gangsters that their killing of each other is so frequent.

We wish to make these points clear: first, that no human society of any kind can continue to exist without some degree of mutual confidence, good will and responsible brotherhood; second, that the more fully these qualities are developed in

any society the stronger and better that society will be; third,
that by and large these qualities are not "born in the blood,"
but are acquired after birth by association with those who have
them; and fourth, that throughout the ages of human experience the most favorable environment for the development of
these qualities has been the intimate, face-to-face social group
which we call the small community.

Community Is Where You Find It. During the early gold
mining days of the West there was a saying among prospectors,
"Silver lies in veins, but gold is where you find it." That is,
the location of a vein of silver may be predicted, but gold may
occur anywhere. The spirit of community is like gold. While
it is most native to the small face-to-face community, yet it
travels far, and appears in the most unexpected places. Wherever men associate they begin to create limited communities
with characteristics of intimate acquaintance, mutual confidence, cooperation, and often a spirit of brotherhood. I recall
finding this spirit very strong in a migrant camp of "Okies"
in Arizona. It was present to some degree at the sinking of
the Titanic.

Large cities usually are netted with such relationships.
Smaller church congregations, neighborhood groups, labor
union locals, some professional groups, ethnic islands, and
many other city groups show elements of the spirit of community. Neighborhoods of immigrant families may hold together in city environments for generations, maintaining the
spirit of community which they brought with them from over-
seas villages. This is illustrated by a statement by Judge
Samuel Leibowitz of New York: [2]

> Take Chinatown in the City of New York. It is still a community.
> Chinatown has the lowest crime rate in the entire city. Why? Be-
> cause it is still a neighborhood where neighbor knows neighbor.

I am informed that the investment bankers of New York,
in their dealings with each other, are like the neighbors of a
small village. Each is intimately acquainted with the business
habits of the others. Transactions involving millions of dol-
lars are conducted over the telephone, perhaps with no other
record or contract than a brief memorandum of the terms.
Should any member of the investment banking community fail

to maintain the banking community standards, he would no longer be recognized as a member of the community.

In industrial America there are numerous groups of fairly large manufacturers in fields so limited in size that every industry in each field, and nearly every possible customer, knows every other. In the manufacture of paper mill machinery, for instance (which I take on a chance, for I know nothing about it), I should expect that, since there are very few firms in the field, and relatively few customers, the product of every such company would be quite intimately known to every other and to nearly all possible customers. One would expect a high degree of integrity and mutual confidence in that industry, and a tendency to eliminate those who lacked that quality.

There is something very deep, perhaps in the inborn traits of men, and at least in the cultural tradition, which, when conditions are favorable, will respond to good will and confidence. Quite commonly in such cases the practice of competition is tempered and humanized, though not eliminated.

Community as a Localized Population Group.   We have discussed community as a spirit. The other meaning we are concerned with is as a small, localized social unit. During most of human existence such population groups, usually in the form of villages, have been the nearly universal settings of human life. Probably more than 99% of all men who have lived have been villagers. Men have been so deeply identified with this way of living that few societies have long survived its disintegration and disappearance. Man is a small community animal.

While these small population units have not been the sole possessors of community qualities, yet some living conditions and circumstances are more favorable than others for keeping alive that spirit. The many urban associations, while of great value, usually are poor substitutes for full community life, especially as to opportunity for children to learn the normal processes of living by sharing life and experience with their elders. Community as a quality of life has depended much on community as a small, localized population group. When we speak of community we commonly mean these two elements in association.

What Is a Typical Community? The two most fundamental
social units are the family and the community. Most sociologists would agree that this is true, at least so far as the
family is concerned, and that to destroy the family would do
irreparable damage and would change the nature of society.
Yet how few actual families are examples of what we think of
as a family at its best! The family is subject to every kind
of distortion, perversion, impoverishment, neglect, dishar-
mony, coldness, disloyalty, stress and suspicion. Its very
possibilities of excellence make it the more susceptible to
injury and distortion, just as many more things can go wrong
with an airplane than with an oxcart.

Yet with all its common disabilities it is an invaluable and
necessary institution. The social aim is not to destroy it, but
to realize its possibilities for excellence. The typical family
is not the average family, but the one which realizes the possibilities for excellence. The same is true of the community.
The typical community is not the battered remains of abuse,
neglect and exploitation, but rather the one which has had fair
approach to fulfillment of its possibilities.

III

The Evolution of Social Controls

Community may have more meaning for us if we realize that it is an inherent and vital part of the age-long human drama, and has been the stage on which most of that drama has taken place. Taking community by itself, outside the course of the human adventure, it may seem to be but one of the social devices men have hit upon, one that may without serious loss be exchanged for other kinds of social organization as convenience dictates. However, viewing it in relation to the course of human life as a whole we can get a sense of its greater import. It therefore is desirable to discuss the evolution of human and social controls as a way to a better understanding of the possible place of the community of the future.

If we limit ourselves to factors commonly recognized in conventional thinking, we may say that in the background of humanity there have been three kinds of controls or guides of attitudes and action. First, we repeat, on the animal level there have been biologically inherited drives, including what we call instincts, some of which continue to powerfully affect human conduct. Second, on the human level there is cultural inheritance or social tradition, which perpetuates and transmits from generation to generation the socially accumulated experience, skill, judgment and wisdom of men. Third and last to appear in the course of human development, there is the process of critical thinking, including conscious inquiry, exploration, research, and in its highest expression, what we call creative thinking. This third element appraises and judges the other controls, and originates new patterns of attitude and action. If we understand the relation of each of these several elements of control to each other and to community life we shall have made headway in understanding both the past significance and the future possibilities of community.

Many people, in the channels of conventional thought and opinion, believe that there is a fourth source of control and guidance of attitude and action. Mention will be made of that subject later.

Animal Drives. As has already been indicated, in all animals except men the general course of life is determined chiefly by instincts and other inborn drives that are inherited with the bodily make-up, and do not need to be learned. In many cases these instincts are marvelously complex and related to particular periods of life. Such inherited biological controls hold their subjects in fairly rigid servitude. An animal has little if any choice as to the instincts by which it will be ruled, though often the manner of their action can be adapted to specific circumstances.   A bird builds its nest because of instinct, but the particular spot it builds in, and the materials it uses, may depend on what are most readily available.

These inborn drives evolve very slowly. If changes in the environment take place so rapidly that the inherited characteristics cannot become adjusted to them through the slow processes of evolution, then the species concerned may fail to survive. Thus for each species existence has been an adventure in living which, according to the fossil records left behind in the rocks, has had relatively small chance of success for that particular species.   Students of evolution are generally agreed that, largely because of the slowness with which biological traits evolve in their adjustment to circumstance, for every species which has survived by successful adjustment, many others have failed and become extinct, leaving no descendants. The number of species that have had their try at life and have failed to survive or leave descendants runs into many, many millions. Yet until recent times—as time runs in the course of evolution—the animal inborn drives, with all their fallibility, were nature's chief reliance for the control of action and attitude in the interest of survival. Nature is not an infallible craftsman. She makes many false moves for one which proves to be successful.

The Emergence of Social Tradition.   In the apparently blind groping of biological evolution through hundreds of millions of years, numberless devices for increasing the possibilities of survival were stumbled upon or were otherwise tried out, many of which proved to be ineffective. We particularly draw attention to two methods for increasing the prospect for survival which have been strikingly successful. One was the development of intelligence, associated with the increase of grey matter in the brain, and the other was the habit of social or community life.

As men evolved in intelligence they were increasingly able to observe when their animal drives were leading them right, and when they were providing misleading guidance, or no guidance at all. Men began to find it necessary or desirable at times to act somewhat independently of their animal drives, or perhaps directly at variance to them. To illustrate by a simple case:

In primitive life men seldom got as much sugar as they needed, and there developed a strong, inborn liking for sweets, which made it more probable that bodily needs would be met. Under present conditions, with sugar abundant as a result of human technology, that inborn craving tends to be misleading. Many people, following their inborn craving for it, eat too much sugar, sometimes with serious injury to health, and making health training in this respect necessary.

But even with increased intelligence, men's inventiveness and insight did not meet their needs. Insofar as it was left to each individual to discover when to follow his instincts or other inborn drives and when to take a course independent of them, very little progress could be made in breaking free from the tyranny of blind instinct. The way out of that difficulty was through the development of *cultural traditions*.

The essence of this second source of control—which goes by such names as mores, culture pattern, social tradition or cultural inheritance—is the passing on from generation to generation of accumulated experience, skills, knowledge, insights, judgment and wisdom. This accumulation of cultural inheritance gradually took the forms of manners, customs, morals, religion and laws. If any certain animal drives should be leading into a blind alley or to conflict or deterioration or threat of extinction, the combined social judgment and wisdom of men, perhaps contributed to through the centuries by exceptionally intelligent and high-purposed leaders, would appraise such trends and would endeavor to point out a better course. Many of these social controls in effect undertook to supersede inborn drives as controls of conduct. They called on men to resist those which the accumulated social judgment held to be disadvantageous to survival or welfare, and to act instead in the manner which society had decided was best.

In every human society life is a disciplined process or it is chaos. The inborn drives have so much faded out that they cease to provide adequate guidance, even on the animal level. In becoming human, man largely gave up his ability to be an effective animal. The social discipline which he has accepted in place of animal drives is not the creation of a generation or of a century, but is the slow accumulation of many, many generations.

For instance, in many species of higher animals an individual will retaliate if injured by another. In most human societies it gradually became the recognized common judgment that it is not in the long-time interest of society for each man to retaliate as he may see fit, and perhaps to avenge a wrong by killing his neighbor. As Francis Bacon expressed it more than three centuries ago: "Revenge is a kind of wild justice, which the more man's nature runs to, the more ought law to weed it out." Society sets up rules to govern retaliation. Because of the strength of the animal impulses involved, the great range of circumstances, and the varying judgments of different societies, the rules and moral standards governing retaliation differ greatly. The common judgment is by no means infallible. Such fallibility will be discussed later.

Nearly all societies, primitive and modern, have concluded that the sex drive requires social control in the general interest. That these social judgments concerning sex are the development of pragmatic conclusions from accumulated social experience is evident from the fact that while there is almost universal recognition of need for control, the types of control in different societies show marked dissimilarities. Many other animal inclinations or drives might be cited which cannot be depended on as guides to action.

Custom and tradition can change much faster than inborn drives. Whereas it might require ten thousand years of biological evolution for an inborn instinct to change to meet changed conditions, a social custom or tradition in primitive life might change in a few hundred years, or under pressure in a much shorter time. With that relatively quick adjustment men became able to live under a greater range of conditions, and more in harmony with their long-time welfare, than can any other animal.

Also, by perpetuation of skills and crafts through cultural tradition, great improvements could be made in the arts of living, and limitations of environment could be overcome. If the climate was too cold men could make fires, wear clothes, and build houses. If wild food failed they could plant gardens and domesticate cattle. Even for very intelligent men it would have been impossible to invent these arts anew in each generation. They could be perpetuated only through cultural continuity. Throughout countless generations the small community or village was the medium in which that tradition was maintained. Cultural evolution, so far as its basic elements are concerned, has been largely a community process.

As the cultural tradition gradually accumulated and became more dependable, and as men slowly acquired an increasing degree of traditional judgment and wisdom concerning when to follow an inborn animal drive and when to resist its dictation and take a better course, the social inheritance tended to assume greater authority over men's actions and attitudes. Inborn animal drives lost much of their grip on the direction of life, and became steadily weaker. Many animal drives quite died out; so much so that some psychologists have held that modern man has no instincts.

Men are much more the product of cultural tradition, and much less the product of instinct, than generally is supposed. As indicated earlier, we know that while a child learns the mother tongue almost unconsciously, whether he learns Chinese or Arabic or English or some other language will depend, not on his inborn nature, but on the language of the group in which he grows up. Should he have lived entirely among deaf-mutes he would not have learned any language. Similarly, whether a child learns good will, considerateness and mutual helpfulness will depend largely on whether those traits prevailed in the society in which he grew up, and on whether his associations were sufficiently intimate for him to acquire them by example and imitation. Yet some inborn drives, especially the more elemental and deeply rooted, survive with varying degrees of vigor; and some of them, such as hunger, caution, sex attraction and maternal affection, are still necessary or useful in the conduct of life.

Animal drives and social traditions share, and sometimes compete, in the guidance of human attitudes and action. Because of ever-changing circumstance, and the fallibility of human tradition, judgment and motives, these controls of custom, law, etc., are not fixed and stable. That instability is seen in the conflicts and differences of judgment in human affairs.

As compared with control by instinct and other inborn animal drives, the control of life by social tradition has been a greatly liberating influence. In over-all effect, the transition from extremely slow-changing instinct to relatively quick-changing social controls not only freed men from the dictatorship of instinct, but greatly enriched human life. Such social qualities as integrity, loyalty, considerateness and mutual helpfulness, some of which probably had their origins as animal drives, could be socially recognized, approved and encouraged, and passed on to succeeding generations by the contagion of example and by other expressions of the social tradition. Thus such qualities became enduring social ideals.

The Community's Part in Social Tradition.   We have mentioned two dominant and interacting factors in the evolution of cultural tradition on the human level. These are *intelligence* and *community*. Cultural tradition is not solely a human possession. In many species of social animals it is a product of social living.

We have but vague ideas as to how much other species depend on social tradition, or how handicapped they would be if the cultural chain should be broken. It is probable that among gregarious higher animals there is more dependence on this continuity of social learning than is commonly recognized. Robert Yerkes, working in his "primates laboratory," found that a chimpanzee, naturally a community animal, when brought up in isolation from others of its species, was quite at a loss when she had a baby. She was afraid of it, did not know what to do with it, and wanted to run away from it. If she had grown up in chimpanzee community she would have learned about motherhood from the common community life.

While many animal species do maintain cultural traditions, yet limitation of intelligence has prevented other than the human species from taking more than very limited advantage of their possibilities.

Quite obviously, the method of passing on accumulated experience, skill, judgment and wisdom of the past is a *social* process. To some degree it has been effective within single families, but that was too narrow a base for its full effectiveness. From long before our ancestors were human they lived in little societies, in what the sociologists call primary-group or face-to-face communities. Our nearest biological relatives, the primates, similarly live in small social groups, each species in communities of a size natural to that species.

As to the universality of this type of human social organization we quote Murdock in his *Social Structure*,[3] a report of the ten-year Cross-Cultural Survey of the Institute of Human Relations of Yale University, which included a study of 250 human societies of many sizes, times and localities:

> The community and the nuclear family are the only social groups that are genuinely universal. They occur in every known human society, and both are also found in germinal form on a subhuman level. Nowhere on earth do people live regularly in isolated families. Everywhere territorial propinquity, supported by divers other bonds, unites at least a few neighboring families into a larger social group all of whose members maintain face-to-face relationships with one another.

While the social controls, and the social skills, manners, morals and laws which pervade all human societies must have originated in small-community relationships, the fairly general custom of mating outside the home community, as well as trading and other intercommunity relationships, led to the dissemination of common cultures over considerable areas. The more completely separated and isolated the races and societies have been, the more varied are their cultures. Yet, because human nature is fundamentally alike everywhere, and because life everywhere presents many similar problems, there tend to be many similar elements of cultural tradition even in the most widely separated societies.

It has been largely in the small community, where more than 99% of humanity have lived, that the fundamental elements of the cultural tradition have grown. The familiar relations of family and community have provided the most favorable conditions for the development of fundamental human culture. During the many thousands of years of human and near-human community living, while the cultural tradition was more and more asserting control over human affairs, even the biological inheritance with its inborn animal drives was being modified by community living and adjusted to it. In fact, men did not create community, but community created men. Our remote ancestors became human by living in community. For instance, speech could develop only in social groups, and *physical* evolution *in society* made the vocal cords into more excellent instruments of expression. Hairlessness of the human body could develop only when the making and wearing of clothes had become so dependable an art that natural hair or fur could be dispensed with as inferior, and this must have been the outcome of a long-continued traditional social process. Thus *cultural* inheritance has acted upon and modified *inborn* traits. Most characteristically human or "humane" qualities are products of small community life, even if now they have come to be inborn. Man is very definitely a small community animal. A normal small community is not just a collection of persons living closely together and having some activities in common. It is a living, vital, social organism, with a life and character of its own.

In this development of the cultural inheritance, communities of small size had several advantages. In primitive life the number of persons in a village might be limited by the available food supply. But there are more fundamental reasons for limited size. The small community made possible very intimate personal acquaintance. Since each member knew every other member thoroughly, deceit became ineffective, except for deliberately secret cults, as of medicine men or priests. Out of this general intimacy grew mutual confidence, the first requirement for the existence of society. Young children need not fear any member, and in that mutual confidence there developed good will and good citizenship. The small community was like a large family, with each member sharing good or ill fortune with the rest.

Carefully controlled observation has disclosed that infants develop much more normally if they have physical contact and the personal affection of the mother than if these are lacking, and that the mother's mental and physical development benefits from the same relationship. Similarly the intimate personal relationships of the face-to-face small community actually do count heavily in development of mutual trust and regard, and the quality of the common life depends largely on the degree to which this element of community is present, especially for children.

The essence of human society is the emotional quality which goes by such names as social responsibility, mutual confidence and affection. This is an element of cultural inheritance. It is stronger and freer from counterfeit and adulteration in some societies than in others, and in some segments of society than in others. When the seed of that cultural inheritance is planted in an individual he can increase it by nurture or kill it by neglect This quality originated chiefly in small community relationships, and has had most of its encouragement and development there. In the absence of some kind of community it fades, and to the extent that it does fade, society deteriorates or disintegrates. This spiritual quality, which we may properly call "community," is essential to the human adventure.

Some Limitations of Cultural Inheritance. Important and determining as the cultural tradition has been in human affairs, and important as it continues to be, it has serious limitations. Its very importance in time came to create a form of servitude. As inborn animal drives lost much of their firm hold on conduct, and tended to weaken or to disappear under the growing dominance of the cultural tradition, and as that tradition came to be the chief source of control of action, it became so important, in fact, that no human society could survive without it. A break or serious deterioration in the social tradition might be disastrous.

As a natural result of this dependence, the preservation of unmarred cultural tradition became almost the highest virtue.

It may have taken a thousand years for a primitive society to perfect the shape of an arrowhead. It would be the spirit of the ancient culture that such art and precise skill must not be lost or debased. The most meticulous conformity to custom was required. Similarly, to hold in control the slowly and imperfectly achieved mastery of a deep-rooted and powerful animal drive, such as the craving for revenge or the sex impulse, required eternal vigilance.

So, for the welfare of society as a whole the ways of the fathers were entrenched and strengthened by every possible means. Departure from custom was looked upon as the greatest crime. Social traditions which might be endangered by existing powerful animal drives or by undisciplined self-interest, and so were in need of protection, were presented to the people as sacred, given by the gods. This has been a fairly general practice of mankind. Through the centuries such beliefs became very deeply entrenched. Nearly every primitive culture—and many of today's cultures have primitive elements—believed in the divine source of its social codes. Orthodoxy was virtue; heterodoxy was sin. The small community, chief carrier of the basic cultural tradition, was a conserver, but in general did not question or create.

In some primitive societies it became apparent that this uniformity of thought and action was not always good, and in such societies innovation was sometimes welcomed. Yet the largely isolated small community was not a favorable setting for the emergence of new ideas and outlooks. New ideas commonly result from efforts to meet new problems, or to understand and to harmonize contrasting or conflicting ideas. Even if there is freedom to inquire, as among the Eskimos, in a small, closed community where there are uniform patterns of thought and action, such uniformity is so impressed on a growing child that it seldom occurs to him to think or to act differently.

Our socially inherited cultural traits are not all good. Often they include superstitions, bad habits and mistaken judgments which may have been passed on for many generations. Some societies become so loaded down with burdensome superstitions and folkways—often the product of some mistaken generalization from experience, or rules that once were good but

are no longer applicable—that the process of living becomes
a heavy, dull burden.   Some African tribes are so saturated
with belief in evil spirits, evil magic and taboos that a large
part of life is spent in trying to outwit those imaginary evil
influences.

In India the expense of ostentatious marriage customs may
consume the greater part of the family resources. In America
expensively ostentatious funerals are a remnant of barbarism.
Over a considerable part of the world, including the West, the
urban and imperial tradition of totalitarian religious dictatorship, supported by claim of divine appointment, holds many
millions in spiritual vassalage. Family, community and national feuds, which may persist for centuries, also are parts
of the cultural inheritance. The drunken Roman Saturnalia,
continued as the conventional New Year's festivity, has an un-
broken—urban—tradition of more than two thousand years.
Cultural traditions tend to perpetuate the helpful and the harmful together.

In their halting and fallible efforts to understand their world,
and to give continuity to that understanding through their cultural traditions, men have made many mistaken generaliza-
tions. Because our animal drives often play us false, many
pious men reached the conclusion that all animal drives are
inherently evil. They speak of "the world, the flesh and the
devil." As the Elizabethan poet expressed the prevailing view,
men are: "Born under one law—to another bound." Charles
Kingsley is authority for the statement that in the early Christian centuries, when Egypt was solidly Christian, in the presence of the dissolute customs then prevailing in the Mediter-
ranean world there was this assumption that animal drives
are essentially evil. He wrote that half the population of Egypt
were celibates, living in monasteries and nunneries. Thus in
arbitrarily condemning biological drives they were effectively
cutting off those family lines in which there was a strong religious sentiment. They had not discovered that the problem
was not to displace one source of the management of life by
another, but rather to put them in right relations.

The Critical Faculties.   We have now referred to two of
the three controlling factors which, according to conventional

thinking, influence human development and survival: first, the inborn animal drives, including instinct; and second, the cultural tradition. The third and newest factor, which is playing an increasingly important part in human affairs, is that of conscious critical inquiry and exploration, with reason and reflection, including as its highest expression what is called creative thinking.

We have noted that conservatism was a dominant characteristic of early village society. As communication and understanding increased, bringing possibilities for more rapid evolution of the cultural tradition, the spirit of conservatism opposed such changes. That attitude of resisting change has been a powerful influence in most societies, but especially in the indigenous small community. Most such communities the world over are still conservative, holding somewhat undiscriminatingly to the old, both good and bad.

The result is that in modern life the traditional culture of itself is not sufficiently sensitive to changing conditions, and to increasing intelligence and knowledge, to be an adequate guide. It often takes too long to depart from the ways of the fathers and to successfully meet new conditions. Inquiry and exploration, with readiness to examine old ways in the light of new conditions, commonly has been inadequate in indigenous small communities.

Cities are the meeting places of widely different cultures, ideas and loyalties. Similarly, seafaring traders commonly are meeting people quite different from themselves. As persons of many different cultures live together in cities or meet in the ports of the world they are compelled to adjust to each other's different outlooks and standards. Tolerance emerges. This tolerance attracts persons of inquiring mind, and they come to prefer that environment to the relatively rigid conformity of the typical small community. As exceptionally active minds associate in cities they stimulate each other, sometimes bringing about great cultural advance. The loosening of traditional patterns of action makes possible quicker adjustment to changing circumstances and the taking advantage of more possibilities.

Because urban life has such marked and obvious values it has been unconsciously assumed in most parts of the world that those values are the important and controlling ones. It is partly for that reason that, as we have said, the flight from tradition-bound village to free-thinking city has been worldwide. Yet some of the qualities of character and attitude which give society strength, stability and refinement are neither inborn animal drives nor are they the products of the critical reasoning of the present generation. They are part of the traditional cultural inheritance.

Such traits as social responsibility, mutual confidence and regard, friendship and good will, while justified and supported by logical thinking, have a large emotional element. Having evolved through many thousands of years by the slow accumulation of experience and insight, they are aroused anew in each generation by the contagion of intimate personal contact and by largely unconscious imitation. We learn them as a child learns affection from its mother, by being present and by participating where they have expression, and so acquiring them almost unconsciously.

Logical approval of such traits is very different from their emotional expression. An intelligent, "well-informed" person may learn about a sense of brotherhood and yet never experience it. Such experience is not acquired chiefly by reasoning, but by contagion from those who feel it. To use a Biblical expression, "We love him because he first loved us."

The small community has been characteristically the carrier of this element of the cultural tradition. But it has tended to carry desirable and undesirable elements along together without discrimination. The same community which transmits the tradition of love and brotherhood within its own limits may carry a bitter feud with an adjoining community for generations, even after the original cause has been forgotten.

Just as the change of control from the tyranny of inborn animal drives to cultural tradition was a liberating process, enabling quicker and more effective adjustment to changing circumstances, so also the attitude of questioning, testing, and exploring, and of initiating new attitudes and actions, provides a degree of liberation from too great bondage to relatively fixed traditional culture. Elements of cultural tradition which prove to be incongruous or obsolescent, by the process of critical appraisal may be changed or discarded, and other elements necessary to a consistent whole may be added or encouraged. Wholesomeness of living and unity of personal and social character may be approached, and a larger pattern of thought and action achieved.

Finally come the critical faculties of free inquiry, reflection, exploration, appraisal and experiment. By this new level of action men can discipline and master their cultural inheritance, accepting or rejecting its control as inquiry and judgment may determine. Yet all these levels of action are interrelated. A living man in his body obeys the chemical and physical laws of the inorganic world; his living processes are served by inborn biological drives, and he could not exist without them; as a man he lives largely by the cultural inheritance of the society in which he moves, and finally comes the still higher control of free inquiry. It is the wisdom of life to make harmony of all these.

Just as it is fortunate that such animal impulses as hunger, thirst, a tendency to caution, maternal affection and sexual affection did not disappear, but remain to serve us, though under the discipline of the cultural tradition; so it is fortunate that traditional culture persists in the face of logical reasoning, especially in order to keep alive fundamental values such as good will, mutual regard and mutual responsibility. The attitude of free, critical inquiry constitutes an additional and extremely valuable resource for the management of life. The problem, we repeat, is not to choose one or the other, but to achieve the best division of influence between them.

The Conservatism of the Cultural Tradition. The stubborn conservatism of the cultural tradition, especially as it persisted in small communities, has preserved precious values which otherwise might be lost. For instance, the once new world of feudalism and empire seemed to sweep away the past and to usher in a new kind of society based largely on power and strategy. But the ancient conservative spirit of community democracy stubbornly persisted. In the small communities of mountain fortresses such as those of Switzerland, and in isolated Iceland, but particularly in small communities close to the soil the world over, the old democratic ways persisted until their value was rediscovered.

The cold, cynical philosophy of power and empire, with reliance on strategy, subterfuge and coercion, seems to have become dominant with the rise of mass society, urbanism and regal and military power. It was codified two thousand years ago in India in the work known as *Kautilya's Arthasastra*, in Italy fifteen hundred years later by Machiavelli in *The Prince*, and still later in Soviet strategy, which present-day United States diplomacy seems to be trying to imitate. That code seemed to have taken the world. I have heard more than one quite prominent American official state that in international relations the sole control of policy and action is absolute, cold self-interest, without regard to ethical considerations. A similar attitude often has existed in domestic affairs. In years past the president and founder of a great American industrial corporation, in advising a course of unqualified self-interest, said bluntly, "A corporation has no soul." In the process of "the survival of the fittest," fitness could mean only power to survive, or in short, it meant *power*. All other values would be subordinate.

Yet the stubborn, close-to-the-soil spirit of mutual confidence and good will persisted. By the maintenance of their ancient cultural tradition through the centuries, men of small communities, close to the soil, have stubbornly held to the ancient pattern of human equality, sincerity, dignity, good will and brotherhood. It was in a country dominated by a feudal and regal spirit of human exploitation that Robert Burns, himself a peasant farmer, describing a humble peasant home, wrote in "The Cotter's Saturday Night":

> From scenes like these old Scotia's grandeur springs,
> That makes her loved at home, revered abroad;
> Princes and lords are but the breath of kings,
> "An honest man's the noblest work of God."

and again, in words that might have been written by a present-day cultural anthropologist:

> For thus the royal mandate ran,
> When first the human race began,
> "The social, friendly, honest man,
>   Whate'er he be,
> 'Tis he fulfils great Nature's plan,
>   And none but he!"

In these four short lines we have the essence of the spirit of the old community.

The spirit of ambition for power as expressed in "practical politics" through the ages is typically illustrated in the writings of Machiavelli. The following from *The Prince* is in striking contrast to the spirit of the ancient community as expressed by Robert Burns: [5]

The experience of our own times has shown that those Princes have achieved great things who made small account of good faith, and who understood by cunning how to circumvent the intelligence of others; and that in the end they got the better of those whose actions were dictated by loyalty and good faith. . . .

A prudent Prince neither can nor ought to keep his word when to keep it is hurtful to him and the causes which led him to pledge it are removed. If all men were good this would not be good advice, but since they are dishonest and do not keep faith with you, you, in return, need not keep faith with them; and no Prince was ever at a loss for plausible reason to cloak a breach of faith. . . . He who has best known how to play the fox has ever been the most successful.

It is necessary, indeed, to put a good colour on this nature, and to be skillful in simulating and dissembling. But men are so simple, and governed so absolutely by their present needs, that he who wishes to deceive will never fail in finding willing dupes. . . .

(The following is expurgated from some translations of *The Prince*, perhaps in the very process of carrying out Machiavelli's counsel: "One recent example I will not omit. Pope Alexander VI had no care or thought but how to deceive, and always found material to work on. No man ever had a more effective manner of asservating, or made promises with more solemn protestations, or observed them less. And yet, because he understood this side of human nature, his frauds always succeeded." —A.E.M.)

It is not essential, then, that a Prince should have all the good qualities which I have enumerated, but it is most essential that he should seem to have them; and I will even venture to affirm that if he has and invariably practices them all, they are hurtful, whereas having the appearance of them is useful. . . .

A Prince should be very careful never to allow anything to escape his lips that does not abound in the above named five qualities, so that to see and to hear him he may seem all charity, integrity and humanity, all uprightness and all piety. And more than all else is it necessary for a Prince to seem to possess the last quality. . . . Everybody sees what you seem to be, but few really feel what you are; and these few dare not oppose the opinion of the many, who are protected by the majesty of the state; for the actions of all men, and especially those of Princes, are judged by the result, where there is no other judge to whom to appeal. Wherefore, if a Prince succeeds in establishing and maintaining his authority, the means will always be judged honorable and be approved by everyone. For the common people are always taken by appearances and by results, and it is the vulgar mass that constitutes the world, only the few finding room when the many have no longer ground to stand on.

This conflict between the ethics of community, as expressed by Robert Burns, and the ethics of power as expressed by Machiavelli, is of long standing. Isaiah was referring to Machiavelli's tribe when he wrote, 2000 years before the Italian:[4]

> Woe to those who join house to house,
>   who add field to field,
> until there is no more room,
>   and you are made to dwell alone
>   in the midst of the land.
>
> And who say, "Who sees us? Who knows us?"
>   You turn things upside down! . . .
> The way of peace they know not,
>   and there is no justice in their paths;
> they have made their roads crooked,
>   no one who goes in them knows peace.

But the Isaiahs, like Robert Burns, were certain that "great nature's plan," or in Isaiah's mind, God's plan, was very different from the regime of power and strategy then dominant, and would prevail:

> The knaveries of the knave are evil;
>   he devises wicked devices
> to ruin the poor with lying words,
>   even when the plea of the needy is right.
> But he who is noble devises noble things,
>   and by noble things he stands. . . .
> For the palace will be forsaken,
>   the populous city deserted; . . .
>
> Then justice will dwell in the wilderness,
>   and righteousness abide in the fruitful field.
> And the effect of righteousness will be peace,
>   and the result of righteousness,
>   quietness and trust for ever.

He who walks righteously and speaks uprightly;
he who despises the gain of oppressions,
who shakes his hands, lest they hold a bribe, . . .
He will dwell on the heights; . . .
his bread will be given him, his water will be sure.

For long centuries during the reign of ambition, power and oppression, this cultural tradition of the ancient community, the tradition of sincerity, good will and mutual confidence persisted against the seeming weight of the evidence, and the then current control by ruthless power. We get a hint of the great age of that community tradition from the comments of the arctic explorer Vilhjalmur Stefansson concerning the Eskimos of the Coronation Gulf region. He wrote: "In culture the Gulf Eskimos went back not thousands but tens of thousands of years, for they were just emerging from the age of wood and horn into the earliest age of stone." From Stefansson's long description of the traits of these primitive small community people a few extracts will give a hint of their nature:[6]

Among the Eskimos of northern Canada there was no law except public opinion. . . . Although no one had authority, each person had influence according to the respect won from a community which had intimate knowledge of everybody. . . . With the primitive Eskimos every debt was a debt of honor; for there were no police, judges, prisons, or punishment. . . . The same force which compelled the Eskimo to pay his debts compelled him to do his share of the work according to his recognized abilities. I never knew even one who didn't try his best. . . . If there had been a shirker, he would have received the same food; but, even in a circle of punctilious courtesy he would have felt that he was not being fed gladly. . .

The successful man stood above his fellows in nothing but their good opinion. The skillful hunter did not have better clothes than the poor hunter. . . . Your importance in the community depended on your judgment, your ability, and your character, but notably upon your unselfishness and kindness. Those who were useful to the community, who fitted well into the community pattern, were leaders. It was these men who were so often wrongly identified by the careless early civilized traveler and the usual trader as chiefs. They were not chiefs, for they had no authority; they had nothing but influence. People followed their advice because they believed it to be sound. . . .

Fortunately we do not have to debate whether little-civilized and uncivilized Eskimos are the happiest people in the world, for most travelers have agreed on their being the happiest, or at least seeming to be. . . .

On the basis of my years with the people of the Age of Stone, I feel my vote will have to be that, while there may be some rightness about some of the other explanations, the chief factor in the happiness of the Stone Age Eskimos was that they were living according to the golden rule.

For how long has this antithesis between power and good will been in existence? We have no clear evidence. It perhaps began when men first assembled in large masses, say ten thousand years ago, and not everyone in the community could know everyone else. Where large numbers of people were involved the condition arose which is described by Machiavelli: "Everybody sees what you seem to be, but few really feel what you are, and these few dare not oppose the opinion of the many, who are protected by the majesty of the state." Under such conditions, so far as survival is concerned, as Machiavelli stated, "It is not essential that a Prince have all the good qualities, but it is most essential that he should seem to have them." In other words, intrigue, make-believe, hypocrisy— many forms of dishonesty—come to have survival value, which they did not have in the primitive small community where everyone knew everyone else.

For how long will dishonesty and crude power in their varied forms continue to have survival value? Perhaps until the spirit of community can again become dominant.

As an indication that the spirit of Machiavelli was not born with him, and that its fruit never was entirely sweet, we shall quote from another of the same school who lived in India at about the beginning of the Christian era, or perhaps two or three centuries earlier. The author, Kautilya, if the record is to be credited, also was a consultant and adviser to a very powerful king. The adviser is outlining the "Institution of Spies":[7]

> Assisted by his prime minister and his high priest, the king shall by offering temptations, examine the characters of his ministers. (Then follow detailed instructions for spying on them.—A.E.M.)
>
> Assisted by his council of ministers tried under espionage, the king shall proceed to create spies: spies under the guise of a fraudulent disciple, a recluse, a householder, a merchant, an ascetic

practicing austerities, a classmate or a colleague, a fire-brand, a poisoner, and a mendicant woman. . . .

Having set up spies over his prime ministers, the king shall proceed to espy both citizens and country people. . . .

Having secured his own safety, first from his wives and sons, the king can be in position to maintain the security of his kingdom.

As to how to "maintain the security," one of many similar advices may be cited:

A spy may instigate the brother of a seditious minister, and, with the necessary inducements, take him to the king for an interview. The king, having conferred upon him the title to possess and enjoy the property of his seditious brother, may cause him to attack his brother; and when he murders his brother with a weapon or with poison, he shall be put to death in the same spot under the plea that he is a parricide.

Such is the normal fruit of a policy of "enlightened selfishness." For so long as enlightened selfishness is in control, "common-sense" compromises with integrity become necessary. These may call for additional compromises. Where is the end? There is no control of the compromise with integrity except by the prevailing cultural pattern. The closer that pattern is to the fundamental pattern of community in respect to integrity, the higher will be the level of the society.

Some people have thought of Burns as an original genius in writing the lines we quoted earlier, but he was only putting into literary form a conviction commonly expressed the world over by men close to the soil, whose voices seldom rose to the level of literature, except as an Amos or the Isaiahs or a Robert Burns or an Abraham Lincoln rose up from the soil to give expression to that persistent cultural tradition. It was men from close to the soil, clinging to that ancient community tradition of freedom, integrity, equality and dignity, who brought the spirit of freedom to America.

Therefore we can be thankful that there has been conservatism and persistence in clinging to the community pattern of human relations during the long centuries while power and ambition were in the saddle, and seemed to have the greater survival value and to appeal more to "intelligence" and "common sense."

The Spirit of Community. The spiritual quality of community comes chiefly through cultural tradition rather than through logic or critical inquiry. The literature on community in America has been concerned chiefly with the mechanics of living together. As I have observed some very logical community betterment programs financed by philanthropic foundations, but which have been nearly sterile or worse, I have thought of an old bit of doggerel:

> "It is clear, " said William Van Brink,
> "That a poem's but paper and ink;
> Yet I've had them both here
> For an hour, 'tis queer—
> There is something yet lacking, I think."

It is not difficult to see that the physical, economic and social settings of life are important. Physical starvation reduces the quality of life. Being illiterate narrows a man's world to what he physically sees or otherwise experiences, and to the content of the culture immediately about him. It hinders him from breaking through the narrow bounds of local thinking to the lives and thoughts of great men as recorded in literature. Lack of modern sanitation often brings disease and premature death. Bad social and political organization may distort the life of a people.

Yet seldom are the chief limitations of a community those which can be described in physical or sociological terms. Often such shortcomings are the results of others of a more subtle nature. American theory and practice concerning the community, like the literature on the subject, have been largely concerned with physical well-being and with efficient social arrangements. They have tended to produce an excellent social mannikin, without the soul of community. Some prevailing practices go further and tend to destroy any soul which might have been inherited from the family and community life of the past. Among such practices are: the present powerful drive to destroy community experience by school consolidation for young children; creation of mass industries where they are not technically imperative; and the drilling of elementary and high school pupils in the spirit and attitude of war by the use in public schools of army-prepared textbooks, followed in the process of universal military training by drill in the spirit of war. Radio and television programs, as they usually run, constantly incite to desire for more physical possessions and personal indulgences as chief incentives of life. These combined influences are tending to produce in America a type of mind and spirit which can be described accurately as materialistic.

Except as community transcends this attitude, efforts at community development will continue to disappoint their promoters. When universal education was first being presented to our country it was looked upon as the way to prevent delinquency and crime, but these have increased about as rapidly as education. Crime and intemperance were taken to be the results of poverty. Eliminate poverty, we were told, and these evils would largely disappear. But the near elimination of poverty has had no such result.

The spiritual element of community, which primarily is a part of the cultural inheritance, rests on no single quality. As in an individual, it may be strong in one respect and almost fatally weak in others. However, there are a few qualities of a good community cultural inheritance which are so elemental and fundamental that without them the keenest intelligence, the best technology and the most skillful social organization probably will fail. Many years ago a man who had some of the qualifications of a competent sociologist expressed himself concerning one of these qualities. He said: [8]

If I speak in the tongues of men and of angels, but have not love, I am a noisy gong or a clanging cymbal. And if I have prophetic powers, and understand all mysteries and all knowledge, and if I have all faith, so as to remove mountains, but have not love, I am nothing. If I give away all I have, and if I deliver my body to be burned, but have not love, I gain nothing. . . .

Love is patient and kind; love is not jealous or boastful; it is not arrogant or rude. Love does not insist on its own way; it is not irritable or resentful; it does not rejoice at wrong, but rejoices in the right. Love bears all things, believes all things, hopes all things, endures all things. Love never ends. . . . So faith, hope, love abide, these three; but the greatest of these is love.

This passage often is quoted as a beautiful, imaginative piece of poetical expression. To a considerable degree it also is good sociology and good psychology. The occasions for human misunderstanding and discord are unlimited. No government can be so intelligently efficient as to remove all inequality. No tactful management of social relations can prevent all occurrences of inconsiderateness or partiality or misunderstanding. As major causes for feeling wronged or injured are removed it is common for people to become more sensitive to slighter offenses, and the feeling of resentment or injury may be almost as great. Forces which tend to alienate people and to drive them apart are always present. Even without cause for alienation there can be complete absence of attraction, so that members of society may tend to fall apart from each other, like grains of loose sand.

Love or affection has two chief practical functions: first, it does the seemingly impossible in dissolving resentment, jealousy, suspicion and hurt feelings; and, second, it is an attractive force which pulls people together, transmuting them from inert, discrete bodies into elements of a living, social organism. Without some degree of that quality of mutual attraction society tends to crumble into inert or antagonistic individuals, except as men are precariously held together by external authority or necessity, or by the strategy and habits of self-interest.

The quality of community, of which love or affection is an essential element, is, we repeat, not primarily a product of intelligence, but is a combination of inborn animal impulse and of cultural inheritance. Highly intelligent men may heartily dislike each other. Where can lack of natural cohesion among coworkers be more marked than in a research laboratory staffed by intelligent but personally ambitious men who lack mutual regard and affection? Bliss Perry has referred to the machinations of strategy and intrigue at Princeton when Woodrow Wilson and Dean West were pitted against each other, each with intelligence, but without affection.[9]   In contrast I recall a comment by George Herbert Palmer concerning the philosophy department at Harvard where those qualities did exist: "What happiness to work under conditions of entire freedom, where suspicions were unknown, and friendships were profound."[10]

Affection, mutual confidence and regard are emotional, rather than intellectual, qualities, though they may be appraised, judged, and to some extent directed, by intelligence. They originate in part as inborn animal drives, but to a greater degree as part of the cultural inheritance, carried from person to person by intimate contact. Their basis most commonly is laid in early childhood, and in the intimate relations of family, small community or other similar group; yet wherever men gather, in village or city, we see some degree of effort to possess these qualities. Social structure on the local level is important chiefly in the degree to which it provides conditions in which such relationships can thrive. It is fortunate that these parts of our animal and cultural inheritance survive. Critical inquiry could not take their place.

Yet even here the cultural inheritance needs to be informed by disciplined free inquiry. Men constantly seek for some infallible principle of action which can be lived by without the intervention of critical judgment, and without fear of error. By many people, love is taken to be such a principle. It is felt that if one's motive is love, he can make no mistake. Yet even this precious motive, without which society could scarcely endure, is fallible, and may go far wrong without the guidance and discipline of free, critical inquiry. Love as emotion must be guided and disciplined by love as intelligent purpose. Such intelligent purpose calls for exercise of the critical faculties.

Sometimes the undisciplined emotional love of a mother for her child has led her to prohibit an operation necessary to correct what otherwise would be a lifelong defect, because she could not endure the thought of the child undergoing the temporary suffering the operation would cause. Often confidence in the undisciplined emotion of love on the part of kind-hearted parents leaves children so undisciplined that they become lifelong nuisances to society, out of harmony within themselves.

Often the emotion of family love is so strong that a man for love of his brother will help him to secure a position for which others are more competent. That manner of action is called nepotism.

Emotional love of country—patriotism—often is a powerful and desirable drive in men's lives. But it, also, needs the illumination and discipline of free inquiry in relation to total life purpose. When Stephen Decatur, who had expressed his love of country in heroic action, said: "My country, right or wrong, "[11] he simply gave expression to a very old attitude common to indigenous social groups, especially to small communities, the world over. It probably is in part by animal instinct and in part by cultural tradition that when a social group is threatened from without it closes its ranks and faces the menace as a unit, quite regardless of the merits of the situation. In primitive times this attitude contributed to community survival, and it still does to some extent; but there are few social sentiments that are more generally played upon and exploited by self-seeking ambition. Under present world and regional conditions of interrelationships, such uninformed and undisciplined provincial patriotism, no matter how sincere, may be a major cause of war. Characteristically the small community has been susceptible to this weakness.

Complete control of life by cultural tradition would perpetuate the helpful and harmful together, and often would leave the way undefined. Complete control by conscious reason would leave undeveloped the priceless resources of emotional commitment, such as friendship, family affection, group loyalty and patriotism. Should the thread of cultural tradition as to these traits be completely broken, they would disappear except as they would be sustained by inborn animal drives, and society would largely disintegrate for lack of the emotional ties which transmute individuals into society.

Sometimes the deep-seated emotional sets of animal drives or of cultural tradition may be truer guides to living than are the immature results of logical thinking. As Homans wrote in *The Human Group:*[12] "Intellectually, the descent into hell is easy. One false step, and logic will do the rest." And again: "Sophistication includes knowing when not to be sophisticated. No one is more a creature of fashion than the average intellectual." Much "honest," "scientific" thinking has seen nothing ahead for the human race but extinction as the sun grows cold, and in published writings has transmitted the resulting emotional state to the general public.

The optimistic intuitions of men, of both inborn and social origins, probably were a better guide than this immature "scientific" pessimism. It is a sound intuition that we are not justified in setting ultimate limits to human possibilities.

Logic is a recent emergent on the human scene, and is immature and vulnerable. It should increasingly share in the management of life, along with animal drives and with the social tradition, in a spirit of humility, yet with a sense of worth and of social responsibility. The small community, because it is the natural home of the best of our basic cultural traditions, is perhaps the best stage on which to work out the relations to each other of these controls of human action. But to serve that purpose it needs to be freed from the excessive and undiscriminating conservatism which has characterized it in the past.

A Fourth Source of Control and Guidance?   If all three sources of the control and guidance of human affairs which we have discussed—animal drives, cultural tradition and free inquiry—are thus fallible, where, if anywhere, do authoritative, infallible guidance and wisdom lie? Is there some source to which men may turn on which they can place absolute reliance?

Divine guidance is claimed, sometimes for elements of the cultural tradition, and sometimes for phenomena which seem to be nearly identical with creative thinking. Many different cultures hold divine, authoritative revelation to be the origin of parts of their cultural tradition, and with each culture "the faith of the fathers" is held to be the ultimate and infallible authority. These various "revealed" and "sacred" codes are so lacking in consistency and harmony with each other, and each is so obviously the gradual outgrowth of its own particular cultural past, that about all the unquestioning assurance we can have is that the particular revealed code which we were born in or converted to is right, and the others which conflict with it are wrong. "Revelations" seem to have very human origins.

In other cases, as with the Quakers, the expression "divine guidance" commonly refers to a phenomenon which seems to be nearly identical, so far as it goes, with the process which commonly is known in the secular world as "creative thinking." A person gives his best thought to a subject, and then dismisses it from his mind, or prays for light. In the course of time clear judgment, understanding or insight may appear, often without conscious reasoning, and such insight may go so far beyond the results of conscious reasoning as to seem to have another source.

This kind of revelation or "opening" or insight is not confined to people of religious faith. The annals of science record many remarkable examples. For instance, the exceptionally able organic chemist, Kekule, after long, careful thought on the nature of the molecular structure of the benzene molecule —the so-called benzene ring—had a dream in which the atoms of the benzene molecule danced fantastically before his eyes, and finally arranged themselves in a certain orderly way, like a snake swallowing its tail. He recorded this dream, checked it carefully, and found it to have disclosed the true structure of the benzene molecule. His discovery has been called "the most brilliant piece of prediction in the whole range of organic chemistry."[13] Another high chemical authority has stated that "three fourths of modern organic chemistry is directly or indirectly the product of Kekule's benzene theory."

Poincare, sometimes called the greatest mathematician of the twentieth century, and several others, have described similar "openings" in the process of their thinking. In fact, books have been written outlining the steps of that process, which is considered to be a normal action of the subconscious mind.[14]

Most doctrines concerning personal revelations, "openings," and mystic experiences took form before the development of modern psychology and other science. They seem to survive chiefly by avoiding the methods of science to examine their supposedly mystical or supernatural character.

Thus various types of "revelation" have characteristics in common either with the cultural tradition or with creative thinking. In case of creative thinking in science another step is taken than is customary with those who claim revelation; that is, the scientific intuition or "opening" is subjected to rigorous examination and test by the process of critical inquiry.

It seems to be the work and the responsibility of men as best they can to weigh and to judge the claims and demands of these several sources of guidance and control. If men work in sincerity, observing the results of experience, qualifying themselves as best they can for the exercise of disciplined intelligence, laying the basis for sound intuitions, and comparing their findings with each other, it seems probable that overall judgment will become more and more dependable as to the relative parts which should be played by inborn animal drives, cultural tradition and critical inquiry.

So far as seeing and understanding the fundamental values of community, and so far as defining and endeavoring to realize the characteristics of the community of the future, are concerned, that is the course we should commend, and try to follow. We know of no infallible protection from error in that process. The only controls we know are the long-time judgment of men and the discipline of fact and circumstance. Religion, politics, scholarship, personal and social endeavors, in their free play and interaction, are hammering out the shape of human purpose and action.

IV

Must Cultures and Civilizations Disappear?

> The appalling fact is that, after flourishing for a span of time, every civilization but one has collapsed. . . . The one civilization that has not entirely gone to pieces is our own Western civilization, and we are desperately anxious about it. Can it get out of the rut into which the others have fallen?
>
> —Homans, *The Human Group*[12]

The course of history is influenced by a wide range of conditions and occurrences which make the assigning of cause and effect difficult and uncertain. The trend of affairs has been conditioned by geology, climate, plant and animal characteristics, and by human thought and action; also by the retreat of the glaciers, by the drying up of fertile regions into deserts, by plagues and other diseases, by exhaustion of the soil through agricultural practices; by pressure of populations, by inborn human traits such as hunger, fear, and jealousy; by the appearance of men of towering ambition such as Genghis Khan, Alexander, Caesar and Napoleon; by men of great spirit like Buddha, Wyclif, and Gandhi; by the invention of the steam engine and the electric generator and the development of atomic power; and by the thinking of philosophers and dreams of poets.

Through all the confusing and modifying circumstances, we can observe some general trends. One of the unquestionably authenticated uniformities of history is that civilizations and cultures have a tendency to arise from common qualities and circumstances of life, to reach a climax of power and of elaboration of culture, and then to fade or to disintegrate.

Babylon was for a very long time the chief center of western Asia, but only as a continuing site of succeeding cultures, as when the Scythians swept down from the northern mountains and plains, and took over. But even this kind of continuity passed; now the very location of the extinct city is disputed.

Damascus, "oldest city in the world" as to continuous occupation, similarly has not had a continuous culture. At the head of a very fertile small valley, it has been conquered, sacked and repopulated by a variety of cultures, from Persia to Rome and from the Eurasian steppes to Egypt.

Athens, once the center of the world's greatest civilization, almost disappeared, and the culture to which it gave expression survived only in architectural ruins, buried sculpture, or copies of manuscripts. At the beginning of the nineteenth century it was a primitive, largely illiterate village of less than 5000 population.

For about two centuries just before the Christian era Alexandria in the Nile delta was the second city of the world in trade and power, and was far superior even to Rome as a center of science, art and culture. There, more than perhaps anywhere else on earth in ancient times, the frontiers of the human mind were pushed into new territory, especially in science, but also in general culture. Then through the centuries the city sank to mediocrity. When England first entered Egypt, near the beginning of the nineteenth century, Alexandria had shrunk to a town of about 4000. Its art, science and philosophy had long since departed.

Rome developed from communities of hardy, thrifty and virtuous farmers, gradually became master of its own region, then of Italy, and then of a vast territory from the Persian Gulf and what is now southern Russia to the Atlantic, and from the Sahara Desert to Britain. Then Rome shrank to a small town among vast ruins, with a population variously estimated at from less than 10,000 to 30,000.

And so we might extend the list of great cities shrunk to insignificant villages or to heaps of debris—Memphis, Carthage, Syracuse, Timbuctoo, the regal cities of Indo-China whose very existence had been forgotten until their vast remains were come upon in the jungle, and great cities between the Caspian Sea and China that have now disappeared.

Men have long pondered over this succession of greatness and decay. Many have concluded that there is inherent in human societies, as in individuals, a cycle of birth, growth, maturity, age and death. Yet those societies which emerge from primitive simplicity to displace or replace those which deteriorate are just as old biologically as the cultures they displace. It is not human society in essence which exhibits this cycle of growth and decay, but only certain phases of society. If we could clearly distinguish just what it is that leads to cultural decline and death, might we not design and create types of society which would encourage vigor and greatly postpone and decrease decay?

Among the causes of cultural decline there are a few which stand out as dominant. These are, exhaustion of soil fertility, warfare, and decline of personal character. There is a fourth major cause which is not only a direct influence for cultural breakdown, but commonly contributes to each of the others. That is urbanization.

Quite generally, farmers who own their land and live on it take care of it. This is especially true of old civilizations where long experience has developed wisdom about the soil. With urbanization comes the absentee landlord, who cares nothing for his land except to collect rents, and who may seldom leave the city to look at it. A few years ago in India I visited an area which formerly had been well kept and fertile. In recent generations it had been owned by absentee landlords who took a very large part of the crop for rent. They spent the money in the city and did not return enough to keep the tanks (small reservoirs) and irrigation ditches in order. Gradually the cultivated lands shrank to a fraction of what they had been. After taxes and rents the farmers had bare existence, and could not maintain the land. If one did so and had larger crops, his taxes and rent were raised proportionally. This pattern of decadence has been repeated over and over on all five continents.

The second deadly bane to human culture is war. Read histories of empires through the ages and note that they are largely chronicles of warfare, usually of personal or family ambition. A large part of the energies of men, which might have made the earth into a physical paradise, have been consumed in this mutual destruction. War calls endlessly for taxes and soldiers, leaving behind at home poverty and sorrow, and abroad—in case of victory—death, servitude, tribute, and destruction of resources. War is older than history, and in some primitive combats, as tribal wars in Africa before the coming of the white man, sometimes whole peoples were expelled or destroyed. Yet for the most part wars which have impoverished nations and destroyed cultures have been expressions of empire and urbanization.

A third cause of cultural decadence is deterioration of personal character. In its earliest days Rome had a vigorous, thrifty, moral population. The people of imperial Rome, even before the Christian era, had become dishonest, dissolute, and depraved. From what we know of the transmission of cultural traits, we are reasonably sure that this deterioration resulted from the discontinuity of the cultural tradition, which coincided with urbanization and large-scale warfare.

Cultural decline usually has taken place, not in times of national adversity, but in periods of urban and imperial prosperity. The military collapse of a great empire has been like the caving in of a hollow shell. The real causes run back at least for generations. Rural decline often has followed exploitation, conscription, the attrition of warfare, oppression and excessive taxation from the urban centers, or migration to the city. Yet even in face of such causes for decline, village populations may retain their vigor for very long periods.

In Egypt of seventy-five years ago, when long-standing corruption, venality, and intrigue had resulted in disintegration of effective government, and Britain again took over, the "Fellah" population which was distant from cities and from tourist traffic still maintained excellent qualities. Major Sir George Aston,[15] writing of that period, stated: "In the Gordon relief expedition of 1884 the Egyptians did remarkably good work on the line of communication from Assiut to Korti, a distance of 800 miles, and the honesty and discipline of the fellah were shown to be of a high order. By the time of the Omdurman campaign of 1898 the standard of honesty was unimpaired. The large depots of stores at Aswan, Halfa and Dongola could be supervised only cursorily by British officers, and yet when the stores were received at the advance depot the losses were infinitesimal. . . . By nature the fellah is unwarlike. . . . It has been aptly said, 'the fellah would make an admirable soldier if he only wished to kill someone.'"

Another British source of about the same time gives similar testimony. After the conquest of Burma, a British officer, H. Fielding Hall, stayed behind as an administrator and became interested in the country. In *The Soul of a People*,[16] highly regarded by those who knew the old Burma, he wrote of the contrast between central government and rural areas:

It would be difficult, I think, to imagine anything worse than the government of Upper Burma in its later days. I mean by "government" the king and his counsellors and the greater officials of the empire. The management of foreign affairs, of the army, the suppression of greater crimes, the care of the means of communication, all those duties which fall to the central government, were badly done, if done at all. . . . Hardly any official was paid, and those who were paid were insufficiently paid, and had unlimited power. . . .

Outside Mandalay the country was governed by *wuns* or governors. These were appointed by the king, or by the council, or by both, and they obtained their positions by bribery. Their tenure was exceedingly insecure, as any man who came and gave a bigger bribe was likely to obtain the former governor's dismissal and his own appointment. Consequently the usual tenure of office of governor was a year. Often there were half a dozen governors in a year. . . . From the orders of the governor there was an appeal to the council. . . . If a governor sentenced a man to death—all governors had power of life and death—he would be executed long before an appeal could reach the council. . . . The system was rotten to the core. . . .

It may be asked why the Burmese people remained quiet under such a rule. . . . How was it that such a state of corruption lasted for a year, let alone for many years ? . . .

If the government did not do much to help the people, it did little to hinder them. To a great extent it left them alone to manage their own affairs in their own way. . . . And government comes far below other things in importance. A short rainfall for a year is more disastrous than a mad king; a plague is worse than many grasping governors. . . .

In Burma it was only the supreme government, the high officials, that were very bad; . . . all the rest was very good. . . . Each village was to a very great extent a self-governing community composed of men free in every way. . . . Their taxes, for instance, they assessed and collected themselves. The governor merely informed the headman that he was to produce ten rupees per house from his village. The villagers then appointed assessors from among themselves, and decided how much each householder should pay. Thus a coolie might pay but four rupees, and a rice merchant as much as fifty or sixty. . . . So well was this done, that complaints against the decisions of the assessors were almost unknown—I might, I think, safely say were absolutely unknown.

So each village managed its own affairs, untroubled by squire or priest, very little troubled by the state. That within their little means they did it well, no one can doubt. They taxed themselves without friction, they built their own monastery schools by voluntary effort, they maintained a very high, a very simple code of morals, entirely of their own initiative.

These cases might be multiplied many times. In central Europe the personal ambitions, conspiracies, exploitation and loose living of the governing classes, which in the Thirty Years War more than cut in two the population of Germany, still left a peasantry of high quality. Finland, after centuries of domination and aggression and of serving as the battleground of Sweden and Russia, on liberation still possessed a peasantry of exceptional worth.

Not always was the underlying population so resistant to deterioration by the action of a corrupt or decadent elite. In many parts of the world long continued tyranny, war and servitude, or domination by ruthless or decadent rulers, has resulted in deterioration of an entire population, both the ruling class and the villagers. Such conditions must be distinguished from the natural quality of unmutilated small community life. Quite frequently sociologists and others have failed to make this distinction.

By and large the generalization holds good that, except as deeply affected from without or by soil exhaustion, indigenous rural communities may maintain vitality for ages. Social deterioration usually originates with sophisticated urban or official life. We repeat, the often recurring historic cycles of youth, maturity and decay of cultures are not characteristic of human societies as a whole, but only of societies under certain conditions. When a degenerate culture disintegrates and is displaced by a "new" or "younger" or more vigorous culture, the family lines of the "younger" culture have been human as long as those of the degenerate culture which is displaced.

Many years ago, on a Massachusetts hillside, I came across an enormous, exceptionally vigorous clump of royal fern. The clump was three feet across and each of the fronds was four feet high, with a spread of two feet or more. I dug out the entire mass, careful not to disturb the root, and hauled it to Ohio, where I planted it again, but in a limestone soil, which is foreign to its nature. The next year it grew almost as well as in its home ground. Though it lived for several years, each year the fronds were fewer and smaller, until finally the last two or three slender, stunted fronds died.

An urban culture which cuts itself off from the soil of community tends to take a similar course. At first there is little sign of loss. Good manners may take the place of good will, and only a person experienced in community may observe the difference. Openness and integrity may gradually be replaced by tact. Cash transactions become more convenient, and less suggestive of mutual obligation, than neighborly cooperation. Since we have our own friends in club or church or business it really is not convenient to know our neighbors. If we are in trouble of spirit the psychiatrist is available, so we can dispense with the intimate friend. The process would be more rapid but for the fact that the city is constantly fertilized by new arrivals from small communities, and because city populations constantly undertake to provide the equivalent of small communities in various small intimate groups.

If the conditions of social deterioration can be identified and understood, then is it not possible that intelligent purposefulness can so master the human scene as to remove most of them? Insofar as men learn what controls, attitudes and principles of action will produce a good and enduring quality of life, can they not go a long way toward realizing those conditions? The chief limitation of human conditions has not been of power to do, but lack of knowledge and judgment as to what should be done, and of the spirit and purpose to do it.

Perhaps the sequence of youth, maturity, old age and death of cultures and societies, so often observed throughout history, is not inherent in progressive society. Perhaps the normal, vigorous life of societies and cultures may be greatly lengthened, while the principal advantages of metropolitan centers may be retained.

V

The Split Personality of Society

We believe it is sound to consider human conservatism, and its opposite, the spirit of free inquiry and the welcoming of innovation, more as social traditions than as inborn biological traits. In societies where the tradition of conservatism is lost there may be just as much eagerness to change as there is to resist change where that tradition rules. The somewhat extravagant comment in the Book of Acts, "For all the Athenians, and strangers which were there, spent their time in nothing else, but either to tell or to hear some new thing," implies that the conduct of the Athenians was just as natural to them as conservatism would be to a villager.

In discussing the sources of basic cultural traditions we have indicated that most of them had their origins in small communities—villages. Cities have existed for less than one per cent of the life of humanity, and during most of that relatively short period they have held but a small part of the total population. Even at the time the United States became an independent nation less than three per cent of the people of the country were urban.

Under such conditions, intelligence, vigor, leadership and industry were quite evenly distributed through the population. Most of the signers of our Declaration of Independence, and most of the men who drafted the national Constitution, were villagers. They were conservative—harking back to the old days of democracy, before the days of empire. Such distribution of quality was typical of the past. The village was a stabilizing institution. Widely distributed leadership helped to loosen its conservatism; and that prevailing conservatism, in turn, tended to restrain the instability of genius.

We have observed that with the development of cities there was the striking emergence of the spirit of free inquiry and of innovation. The city tended to become a place of free minds, of creative spirits; where questioning, exploring and initiating are not frowned upon. The person of exceptional interest or ability was more apt to find congenial associates there. Culture and power increased together.

It has been a continuing, world-wide phenomenon, from as far back as we have records, that when the free spirit of the city comes into competition with the relatively rigid, unimaginative conformity of the typical, old-time small community, the small community fares badly. This is partly because power, wealth and exploitation usually are at home in the city and operate from it throughout the hinterland. Many people come to the city to escape the poverty which exploitation has imposed on the villages, and if possible to share in the wealth which has accumulated there. That, however, is by no means the only reason for cityward migration. It is partly because the city offers greater freedom and cultural opportunity, and today quite largely because with modern technology a much smaller part of the population is needed for agriculture.

However, this course of urban dominance, as it existed in the past, has had in it the seeds of its own death. While in the small community the stimulation by exceptional personalities is distributed through the population, in the city the concentration of stimulation of such persons by each other goes beyond what the human constitution and human nature can sustain for long periods. The stimulation of competitive industry in present-day America—largely an urban phenomenon—is intense. This, with social insecurity and other urban demands on life energies, has the result that city families generally are short-lived. Six centuries ago Ibn Khaldun,[17] the greatest of medieval sociologists, wrote that in the far-flung Arab Empire urban families died out in about four generations. About a century ago Galton found that to be the case in England, and Havelock Ellis found the same for London of thirty years ago. About 1840 Ralph Waldo Emerson wrote: "The city is recruited from the country. In the year 1805, it is said, every legitimate monarch in Europe was imbecile. The city would have died out, rotted, and exploded long ago, but that it was reinforced from the fields. It is only country which came to town day before yesterday, that is city and court today."

About 25 years ago, with the help of an elderly and especially well-informed businessman, I made a study of the leading industries of Dayton, Ohio, of 35 years before, and of what had become of them. Less than a third of the leading industries of the eighteen-nineties had survived to 1930, and their disappearance was quite commonly associated with the decline or disappearance of the families of the owners.

Various studies based on the 1940 census indicated that in western European and American cities the duration of a city family was no better than the record given for London, and in some cases not so good.

In the controlling matter of biological survival the city always has failed and, at least up to the nineteen-forties, still failed. But for the fact that cities are constantly renewed from small communities, they would soon disappear. This process of attrition of both city and small community, we repeat, may be one of the major reasons why the course of civilization is so much a repetition of climaxes of culture, alternating with widespread decadence.

The city commonly fails to keep alive and strong those elemental traits—of mutual confidence and good will—without which society cannot exist. There is a decrease of all-round trusted friends and neighbors who share the total process of living, and a resulting loss of emotional ties of affection and regard, and of a sense of social responsibility. Out of this lack comes a tendency to breakdown of ethical standards as they are concerned with human relations. As traditional standards tend to dissolve there is a lack of community participation in creating new and better standards. Social disintegration is characteristic of city life, and but for the fact that most city dwellers are but one or two generations removed from the small community this disintegration would be more marked. This does not imply that there are no urban influences which favor the survival of the spirit of community. The medieval guild was such, and the modern city has others. But they are inadequate for the burden put on them.

If the renewal of urban population were from a representative cross-section of the small community or rural population, the results might not be so serious. However, it has been common for the city to attract the extremes of rural and small community life. It receives the ablest, most intelligent, most energetic, and best educated. Also the city is the refuge for the failures and the riffraff from the villages and small towns, who add to city dependency, delinquency and vice. With the disappearance of much of its quality, culture and leadership, the village tends to be left understimulated, flat and unprogressive; the home of honest, neighborly, and industrious, but unimaginative, people. It is poorly adapted to a time when steadily accelerated adjustment is called for.

Of course, cityward migration has been by no means the only cause of the rise and fall of cultures and populations. Other causes, as we have pointed out, are changes of climate, exhaustion of soil fertility, the spread of disease, wholesale migrations and military invasions. Yet, the robbing of rural populations by cities, with the consequent deterioration of both, seems to have been a major factor in bringing many cultures, nations and civilizations to their ends.

The trend has seldom been more active than in America. As Homans comments,[12] "New England's greatest export has always been men, and its most striking monument the abandoned farm. . . . Civilization has fed on the rot of the village."

We have discussed the small community as though it uniformly represented traditional basic culture, and the city as though it lived by a spirit of free inquiry. This, of course, is an oversimplification. Critical inquiry sometimes occurs in old, small-community villages, and various American small communities which have resisted the adverse trends we have described are very much alive and progressive, without having lost desirable small-community traits. On the other hand, most cities are riddled by prejudices, superstitions and taboos. In Asiatic countries I have been startled to observe how the elite can live in the rumbling crater of a social volcano in apparent unawareness and unconcern. Yet by and large the qualities we describe under such names as free inquiry, tolerance and exploration have been more at home in the city, while old, small communities generally are conservative. Despite numerous exceptions and qualifications, the argument in this respect seems sound.

In case an otherwise reasonably healthy man is afflicted with schizophrenia, it may be such a dominant factor in his total life prospects as to command first attention. So the split personality of society may call for major attention, even though it is not the only illness from which society suffers.

The drift from rural to urban life not only has existed at least from old Roman times to the present, but has been greatly accelerated by modern technology. In the past in our country the small community has rested on the American farm. With increasing technology the part of the population needed for agriculture has constantly grown less. When our national constitution was adopted about 85% of Americans were farmers. Today farm families account for only 13 per cent, and the reduction of the farm population never was at a faster rate than during the past five years. Agriculture is now a completely inadequate basis for community. Two thirds of our population live in cities or their suburbs.

The import of this discussion of the split personality of society is that neither the small community as we know it, nor the city as we know it, nor both together as we know them, are adequate to sustain and to promote wholesome, vigorous and stable social culture. If that is the case, what course can be pointed out to cure the illness of society in this respect?

We cannot count on correction coming from the drift of circumstances. So far as natural drift is concerned we are reminded of Tennyson's lines in *In Memoriam:*

> So careful of the type, but no!
> From scarped cliff and quarried wall
> A thousand voices seem to call:
> "I care for nothing: all shall go."

Natural drift has been nature's way of eliminating nine out of ten, perhaps ninety-nine out of a hundred, species of her experiments in living. We know of no divine decree which assures that our civilization and culture shall not follow the course of those many which did ignore the issue, and disappeared from the human scene. It is necessary that we plan our course. The solution does not lie in idealizing the small community or small community life as it has commonly existed; nor in forgetting the problem on the assumption that the life of the city is the life of the future; for seldom if ever has a civilization or a culture long survived the decay and disappearance of its small community life.

Is there any possibility that the small community will again become a dominant or a major part of characteristic American life ? We believe that if a clear picture of the possibilities and values of the small community is given expression, not only in words but in actual cases, the trend to that way of living will grow steadily and rapidly. The flight from the small community has been due in no small degree to its own defects. Especially with the present increase of technology, those limitations are less and less inevitable, while the disadvantages of metropolitan life are becomingly increasingly obvious.

The small community of the future will be neither a replica of the village of the past, nor a surrender to the city. It will be a new creation, uniting the values of both, and largely avoiding their limitations. The attraction of people of excellent quality to small community life when there is a fair chance of fulfilling its possibilities is evidence that it will be appreciated. Any small community of the future which begins to realize its possibilities will be troubled, not by lack of population, but by the fact that too many people will want to come there to live. The best solution of that difficulty is to have many such. The problem of the community of the future is not to win acceptance, but to deserve acceptance. This calls for consideration of every element which enters into the achievement of all-round social health.

Consideration of some of those factors is the subject of Part Two of this discussion.

PART TWO

VI. Foreword

The Characteristics of a Good Community

What conditions of social setting, social and economic arrangements, and attitudes and qualities of mind and spirit favor wholesome and satisfactory living in both city and rural life, and what conditions are unwholesome and unsatisfactory? Is it possible to recognize and to outline those combinations of physical setting, of social and economic organization, and of mind and spirit, which would have most of the advantages of both city and small community, and which would avoid the disadvantages of both?

So far as the potentialities of good society are concerned, modern technology makes this possible as never before in history. It seems that, with a reasonable degree of social stability, in the years to come the physical possibilities of community life will still more greatly increase. With growing knowledge of the nature of human life, both biological and social, the conditions necessary for wholesome living may be increasingly better understood.

If the conditions for wholesome, satisfactory and reasonably stimulating living are generally recognized, then purposeful individuals, families and groups of families, in their free choices in the course of their lives, will tend to make selections which satisfy these requirements and progressively bring them into good relationship.

For the achievement of the best social units or communities there should be: first, the necessary research and other inquiry to find what community and other living conditions and characteristics are most desirable; second, education in social living conditions and other elements of social organization, so that people generally shall be aware of what the values are, and shall have intelligent desire to achieve them; and third, that there shall be developed the necessary skill and habit of actually bringing to pass the desirable conditions. These activities should constitute the social programs of persons and organizations to realize the possibilities of social living.

Given such an approach to the problem, it would seem that the age-old dichotomy of city versus small community can be cured, and that the historic cycles of culture and decadence may largely be transformed into sustained advance. Such a course in some respects will call for a return to the ways of the past, and in other respects a breaking from the past and the design of new patterns of living made possible by advances in technology and by the growing understanding of life and values. Taken altogether, the new community, if we may give that name to the good social unit of the future, may be something new under the sun, yet with the quality of the familiar and the eternal. With such a quest calling us, need life ever have to be afflicted by boredom?

The following chapters deal with some of the elements which may well have our attention when we are considering the community of the future.

VII

A Community Must Have
Necessary Common Functions

Emotional ties between persons do not exist in a vacuum, but
are a function of the activities they carry on together and of the
way these functions are organized. . . . Social disintegration is
marked by a decline in the number of activities in which the members of a group collaborate.

—Homans, *The Human Group* [12]

People do not live together simply to be together. They live together to do something together.

—Ortega y Gasset

It is hard for an empty sack to stand upright.

—Benjamin Franklin

The ancient village was where the people did nearly the
whole of their living—personal, social, economic, religious,
educational and esthetic. The processes of living made occasions for living together. Whenever a part of these are removed from the community its life is reduced.

In exceptional cases some of the finest and deepest friendships originate as purely personal relationships, not brought
about by the proximity or occasion of common calling or other group association. In general, however, men do not make
friendships except where they have had some occasion for as-
sociating. Repeated occasions for acting together enable individuals to see beneath the surface of those they meet and to
recognize qualities which inspire friendship. Also, the very
fact of physical propinquity tends to result in emotional at-
tachment.

The persons who go to a man's funeral usually are those
who were his closest friends. Usually we find them to be persons with whom he had specific, continuing relationships—
his business associates, his fellow church members, labor
union associates or fellow workers, fellow faculty members

or fellow officials. Take away from a man's life those associations which originated in habitual group activities, and in
general there will be relatively few left. Everyday relationships tend to bring about such associations through the whole
cross-section of the small society. The village dweller dis-
covers man's common humanity across all lines of class, calling, cult or creed. Associations are the life of the community.

In modern life there is a tendency to take away from the
community those activities through which men associate. In
olden times men made their living there. Now very many of
them leave the community for factory, store or office at a
distance. In fact, many so-called communities are little more
than lodging places or weekend camps.

One of the greatest vitalizers of community is education.
The community school was a common concern, and nothing
was of more active common interest than the rearing of children. Today, in the passion for more size, more organization,
and more equipment, even elementary school children are
taken from the home environment and required to attend large
consolidated schools, removed from home and neighborhood
life and influence.

Government is best when it is mostly in the community. In
handling relief, health, sanitation, police and safety, local
management calls for participation of community members or
their local representatives. When these functions are taken
away, as when social security is taken over by the national
government, something is—perhaps necessarily—taken out
of the community life. To whatever extent is feasible, the
functions of government should remain in the hands of those
immediately affected—in the community.

Community utilities offer opportunities for common participation. As these are taken away by the State Highway Commission, by the electric power or gas company, the private
water company, and by other organizations, the common life
is impoverished.

In my own little village of Yellow Springs, population 3000,
the operation of the public utilities adds much to the community life and interest. As in most American small towns, the
village operates its own water and sewer systems, cares for
its own streets, and operates its own garbage disposal. In

addition, the village operates its own electric power distribution system, which involves three times as much money expenditure as all the others. In some seasons the village working force is busy with its water or sewer system. At other times the same force is at work on the village streets, or is busy with electric distribution. In case of emergency the whole force is available anywhere in the village. Thus working time is regularized and economized. The same meter reader cares for water and electricity. The villager receives one statement covering water, sewer, electricity and garbage disposal. If local gas distribution should be included in this unified operation the economy and satisfaction would be still greater. The management of these services as part of the function of the village manager makes it economically feasible to have a higher grade of man for that position.

By doing these things together the people become more of a community. The management of such common affairs need not cumber the people of the village with excess of duties and responsibilities. In fact, since the larger volume of common business justifies the employment of a more competent manager and staff, *all* the business of the community may be better handled, and the citizens may be less troubled by details, than though only a skeleton of village functions should be left to the community, with the result that competent supervision could not be afforded. Many a community has dried up and become uninteresting, not because the local people lacked capacity for taking interest and responsibility, but because so many of the natural elements of normal community life have been removed that what remains makes relatively little demand on ability and energy.

In many present-day economic activities there is need for standards of safety and adequacy to be supervised and disciplined by higher authority. Just as the private banking system is supervised by the State Bank Examiner, and the operation of factories by the State Factory Inspector, so local community services may continue to be locally owned and operated, while being supervised and disciplined from above.

Many economic facilities of the community, such as through highways, railroads and post office, must be operated on a scale quite beyond community control. Sometimes control and operation may be divided. Through roads may be administered by the state, and village streets by the community; electric generation and transmission may be owned and administered in large units, with local distribution left to the community. Junior college and university may be state functions, with elementary education largely a community matter, and with high school in between, depending on local circumstances. Always the aim should be to leave local functions in local hands, so far as is reasonably feasible.

In considering characteristics desirable for the community of the future, attention should be given to the need for maintaining community self-reliance and autonomy in as many respects as would be feasible. We repeat, there can scarcely be a small community unless its members have occasions for association and participation, and the more such activities cover the range of common life, the more real will be the life of the community. Some such activity will be public, some private, and some will be in non-economic voluntary associations. In other chapters we have discussed the problems of a degree of economic autonomy for the small community, especially in times of depression or other emergency, and of community autonomy and unity in religious life.

VIII

The Outside Relationships of Communities

Almost no community is wholly isolated from the outside world. In some the contacts are few and infrequent; in other cases the life of the community is so interwoven with that of other communities, societies and organizations that its very individual existence is brought into question.

Frequency and wide range of outside contacts does not necessarily imply a fading of community identity. The Greeks of twenty-five hundred years ago lived largely by maritime trading, and had contacts from Iceland to the southern tip of Africa; yet there was intense and long-continued solidarity of the home villages. Over much of the primitive world inter-marriage of relatives was disapproved, and mating was largely from outside the home community. From ancient times to the present there have been many degrees and great variety of interrelationships. Quite characteristically, though not always, the old-time community survived such interactions, and many of them served to enrich its life. Each person entering a community from outside brought with him or her the general spirit of community, which needed only to transfer its interest and loyalty from one group to another.

In America the circumstances were different. Probably the greater number of towns, villages and neighborhoods were created in the process of the settlement of the country by miscellaneous persons who individually chose to live there. Since there was no community for the first of them to come to, all that came into existence grew out of the spirit of community which the individuals brought with them. This spirit did appear and continue to exist to a considerable extent. Yet, as compared with old, indigenous communities, it often was weak. There was little more thought about the significance of community than there was about the necessity for breathing air; and little realization that the sense of community could die.

Families and individuals moved from community to community and from village or farm to city, unconsciously assuming that the spirit of community was part of human nature, and would be present wherever they went. As the breakdown of community became manifest in increased juvenile delinquency, political corruption, crime, mental ill health and other abnormalities, there was much speculation as to the causes, but only in recent decades has the decay of community been recognized as a major contributing factor.

There has developed in America a habit of free movement of families and individuals from place to place as called for by employment opportunities, educational facilities, relative economic opportunity, availability of farm land, quality of climate and other conditions, quite regardless of the influence of such movement on community life. Such habits have had both good and bad results. Generally they have weakened the cultural tradition. Where the cultural tradition was good, then such moving about has been a disadvantage. Where the cultural tradition has been a narrowing, limiting influence, then that same mobility has had a liberating effect. For instance, in Europe there were many intercommunity feuds, some of centuries' duration. These commonly disappear in America.

In the field of biology and genetics it is considered to be a fairly fundamental principle that the establishing of a new biological type calls for a degree of isolation and also for a degree of interbreeding from outside. Neither alone is adequate for that purpose. In genetics it is understood that the right relation of isolation and intercommunication is of controlling importance.

Similarly, the development and stabilizing of a high type of community calls for enough isolation to allow for the survival and definition of the characteristics to which it aspires, and at the same time enough interrelation with outside life and thought to keep the way open to new ideas and better motivation, and to awareness of the larger whole of which the community is a part. There are great communities and there are petty ones. Too much or too little of either isolation or interrelation, or badly chosen interrelations or interbreeding, may prevent the fulfillment of great purpose for a community. Decisions will come down to practical cases or policies.

For instance, a certain town of about 5000 near the Great Lakes had through three quarters of a century developed a high quality of community life. There was general well-being and prosperity. The internal harmony and self-respect left little for the local police to do but manage automobile traffic. A small part of the community's workers drove to large industries in nearby towns.

Then the town "booster club" became active and, imitating what many booster clubs do, went out to attract an industry to the community. So far as the booster club realized, the selection of an industry required no more discrimination than would be needed in buying a barrel of sugar. The club found an industry looking for a site, and the town subsidized a building for it. It turned out that the management of the industry lacked civic and ethical sense. Instead of employing citizens of the community at the good wages they were accustomed to, the new industry sent to certain southern cities and gathered the slum dwellers easily available, and set a low standard of wages and a very low standard of cheap housing.

Soon the police of the town had their hands full. From the days before the American Civil War when the people of the town had been active in the "underground railway" freeing slaves, relations between the races had been good. With the influx of Negroes from southern slums the good race relations of more than half a century were largely spoiled. The industry and its employees became a chief undesirable element.

What we might call the social eugenics of the community is yet to be fully developed. Many villages and towns with many interrelations are what might be called social mongrels. They have grown by chance, with little sense of direction or aim. A community is subject to the freedom of motion of the population and industry of the country. Sometimes a small town is invaded by an industry it does not want. Yet intelligent purposefulness can have a considerable element of control. There can be more great communities and fewer trivial ones when we learn to give thought to the quality of their interrelationships.

In some degree the spirit of community has survived all the flux of American life. It is not for us to mourn what has happened, but, with a clear idea of the long-time significance of community, to work at keeping and improving what is good and discarding what is harmful, using whatever is desirable from village and from urban life, whatever is good of mobility, and all that is of value in maintaining community roots; and with these elements to create the community of the future. The very flux of America can be our opportunity; it provides a variety of resources and a freedom to design which only rarely comes to a people. That same condition of flux, if not used with insight and purpose, may lead to social decay and disintegration. For without the qualities of community human societies cannot continue.

Cooperation among Communities. The community is such a vital element in the preservation and advancement of a good society that it should be preserved, even at great cost. Yet the day is past in government, economics and other fields in which the small unit can thrive in isolation, or in complete independence. Small units may maintain their normal degrees of sovereignty or independence by cooperation for their common interests. Otherwise large-scale control probably will take over.

In none but the larger cities can merchants and other suppliers make available all the goods and services which their people may need; yet more and more American communities, large and small, are able to provide the greater part of the current needs of their people. They can come more nearly to doing that if adjacent communities develop the habit of cooperating. One community may be particularly fortunate or forehanded in recreation facilities; another may have a clinic and hospital; another may have a junior college; another may maintain an ambitious musical program. Each such activity may add interest and substance to its community, and together a group of communities may provide a particularly good setting for home life. No satisfactory rules can be made for such cooperation. The best preparation is a sensitiveness to circumstances and opportunities. Such an attitude will result in variety, flavor and distinction in the life of a region.

Formal cooperation among communities can be on the basis either of cooperation in specific endeavors, or federation or integration. Where two or more communities unite on the basis of equality, as to provide a hospital, or a recreation area, or a fire-fighting service, or a rural zoning system, to serve their common interests, we have federation. Where to some degree the individual communities give up their individual identities to become elements of a larger unit, we have integration. Both these processes are natural. In case of integration the problem is, how much of independent existence to give up for the sake of common objectives, and how much to retain.

American communities have not shown a great amount of imagination and creativeness in working out forms of cooperation. When some form is discovered it may be widely used, while other equally promising types remain almost undiscovered. Probably the oldest form of cooperation among communities that exists in America is the creation of irrigation systems. Some of the writer's engineering work in New Mexico has dealt with irrigation canals for which there is fairly definite evidence in tribal history of their existence for 800 years. There are thousands of cases of cooperation for irrigation and wet land reclamation. The writer, in serving as engineer on more than fifty such, has observed democratic cooperation at close range.

Suitable legislation can greatly enlarge the possibilities for communities to take such common action. The Ohio Conservancy Act, which the writer drafted many years ago, has proved to be an effective type of such legislation, enabling communities to unite for flood control, parks, water supplies, or certain other purposes, without the intervention of state government. Sometimes cooperation may extend across county or even state lines. It should be the aim of public policy that no such arbitrary barriers as state or county lines should thwart the reasonable desires of communities for varied degrees of federation or integration.

To illustrate another possible field of federation or integration of communities, the Toronto (Canada) Metropolitan Council is a federation and partial integration of metropolitan Toronto and twelve suburban municipalities. Each gave up part of its independence in the common interest, but retained such parts as seemed appropriate to the individual units.[18]

A very different kind of cooperation is seen in the International City Managers' Association. This performs a variety of services for its members, but could do much more.

Groups of communities which cannot each afford specialized services may well set up common service centers for accounting, purchasing, engineering, legal service, planning, equipment maintenance, freight transportation, billing, research on community administration, and other services. If there were hundreds of such regional service associations, they might unite to support an over-all national center for research and for service in difficult cases. If each of the regional associations should periodically report to the general center with statistical and other statements of its costs and activities, comparison of these records would have much the effect of economic competition. The managers of well-run centers would constantly have more favorable opportunities, while incompetent managers, measured by the same criteria, would tend to disappear. Such a type of organization owned and controlled by the individual communities, rather than controlling and dominating them, would be truly democratic, might largely escape political manipulation, and might quite revolutionize small community administration without infringing on the freedom of individual communities.

America has tended to rest on loyalty to the general concept of democracy, and has not used much creative intelligence in discovering how to make it effective in practice. The community of the future will discover and use such helps to administrative excellence.

In the normal, free development of American life, with the help of some creative imagination, we might well expect a much greater variety of types of cooperation, federation and integration to emerge. Craving for uniformity is a characteristic of the mass mind and of mediocrity. Intelligence and imagination seek solutions to fit the circumstances, and since circumstances vary greatly, there will result great variety of cooperation. Quite naturally, some types of action will prove to have general superiority, and will tend to prevail. Thus such uniformity as does emerge will represent inherent superiority, and not blind imitation or inertia.

Full, well-proportioned development does not imply uniformity. An individual can scarcely be said to have all-round, well-proportioned development unless he has become a master in some field. A musician does not become an all-round man by giving up music, but by being a well-developed man as well as a musician.

It is the same with communities. A good community seeks not only balance and proportion within itself, but it will seek to be an effective and valuable element in a larger society. It will seek to have its own unique character, and to make its own peculiar contribution. In a group of adjacent communities the different units may each perform some service which helps the whole to meet social needs. As a large number of individual communities and groups of communities, as part of becoming all-round social units, develop their own unique characteristics and services, they will add to the richness and variety of the total national culture.

Metropolitan Dominance. The major part of the population of the United States is crystallizing itself into relationships which Bogue,[19] in his *Structure of the Metropolitan Community,* refers to as "metropolitan dominance." The metropolis dominates the region about it, such dominance extending to a boundary or twilight zone where the attraction of one metropolitan center is balanced by that of another. Within the range of influence of a metropolis there are subcenters which, while themselves dominated by the metropolis, in turn dominate the area about them. This gradation of dominance extends from the great metropolis down through lesser and lesser centers to the village or hamlet which dominates or serves only the life of the surrounding local neighborhood. In this study, reported by the University of Michigan in 1949, Bogue identified 67 metropolitan centers, containing almost exactly a quarter of the population of the United States. Another 31% were included in 3400 hinterland cities, and another 20% lived in villages or other rural non-farm areas.

This crystallization of the population around the metropolis as a focal point may be either good or bad, depending on its character. Under bad social organization there may be a steep gradient in welfare and in cultural resources from the poverty and drabness of the remote hinterland to the concentrated wealth and luxury of the metropolis. Under a good social organization and modern technology there may be very little difference of culture and economic well-being from the center to the circumference. Educational opportunity may be equalized by social and political policy. Economic opportunity may be considerably equalized by the distribution of industry and its ownership. Cultural opportunities can be largely equalized if the best is made of possibilities of radio, television and other technical developments now existing and likely to emerge soon, and as travel becomes so convenient that there is little inhibition of purposeful association.

In the pre-industrial era the urban metropolis was largely a center of power, luxury and exploitation. Today it is partly that and partly a center of service. To the extent that the elements of privilege and exploitation decrease and that of service increases, the metropolis may be a highly valuable central clearinghouse for specialized services. Its population might need to be only a small fraction of what it is now, congestion might largely disappear, and a larger element of community might be possible within the metropolis.

The advantages of decentralized community living are so great that, given such equalization as we have mentioned, and the elimination of political and economic privilege, communities will more than hold their own.

The Future of Extra-Community Relations. Just as the community includes many groups and associations which contribute to its life and character, and under wise direction may maintain their existence without harm to the community as a whole, so the entire complexity of the larger society will continue to be an interweaving of associations, relationships, interests and organizations—in economics, education, religion, culture, social life and recreation. No fixed rules should be made in general as to the relations of these units to each other, or to the community, the region or the state.

The Nazi and Communist policies of subordinating all such activities to the central control and direction of the state, we believe to be deadly to the general well-being. It was the philosophy of Rousseau that men are born potentially perfect, and are corrupted by the various associations of society. He saw their good traits as natural and inborn and their bad traits as the results of social relations. Hence his famous phrase, "Man is born free, but everywhere he is in chains." To make men free he would destroy the network of associations and would leave only individual man and the supreme state. Then, he believed, the supreme state would protect man's liberty.

Rousseau did not understand that most of the protections of human freedom, no less than its servitudes, reside in its many associations, and that if these are dissolved, then the decision as to who shall control the state will be determined by violence, strategy and conspiracy in the service of personal ambition. He did not recognize that the whole complex of human associations—good, bad and indifferent—make up the fabric of our cultural inheritance. To destroy them all would leave man only a poor grade of animal. He did not see that the problem is not either wholly to keep or wholly to destroy the network of human associations, but patiently, persistently and discriminatingly to remove those threads which destroy the pattern, and to add, reinforce and strengthen those that contribute to its quality.

Rousseau's philosophy led directly to totalitarianism, which, instead of freeing men, made them the instruments of the supreme state, ruled, as he did not realize it would be, by whoever was most ruthlessly successful in ambition for power. Totalitarian dictators, both political and religious, had existed before, and existed in his time, but he did not see that it was their philosophy that he was presenting.

The alternative is to encourage the free play of human associations, controlling them by law only to the extent clearly necessary in the public interest. (The expression "in the public interest" is necessarily without certain definition. Effort to define it and to act on the resulting definition constitutes the proper field of politics, ethics, manners and law.) Then, through the operation of insight, judgment and purpose the more productive associations will be encouraged, and the more destructive ones discouraged. Such a course seems to promise the best type of society.

Yet this free play of nationwide and regional associations tends to penetrate the community and to use attention and resources which otherwise would be directed to community life. Can the community survive this increasing penetration? If the significance and importance of the community are generally recognized, we believe that it not only will survive these influences, but will be strengthened and enlarged by them. For instance, the National Parent-Teacher Association, if it should be "the counselor but not the tyrant" of local thinking, may inform, discipline and enrich the thinking of the local community, and yet not regiment it, or smother adventure or experiment. The same is true of many associations of national or regional interest.

Today some national organizations tend to ignore and to smother the community. For instance, many American communities have endeavored to bring order and proportion into drives for financial contributions, so that these shall be governed by considered judgment rather than by competitive propaganda. Some national health foundations, which make annual drives for funds, have persisted in ignoring and bypassing the community chests of individual communities, and making nationally administered drives in those communities. Their action tends to override the sense of perspective and proportion of the community, and in a degree to destroy the community. The fact that a foundation may return some of the funds to the locality does not repair the damage. There is needed in such cases a realization on the part of the national organization of the significance of the community, and a sense of responsibility to it.

What is needed is not primarily a change of rules but a change of spirit and attitude. In some families parental influences dominate the life and action of children, suppressing or distorting personality. In other families that influence is available for friendship, encouragement, information, and counsel, but without an attitude of either palliation or coercion. So the numberless interrelations and associations which interlace our country may either suck the life out of community and leave it an empty shell, or they may encourage and inform it, and help it to have richness and discrimination which otherwise it would lack. In taking the latter course in relations with communities the various larger associations will be renewing the sources of their own lives.

IX

The Physical Setting
of the Community of the Future

Making the Best of Existing Community Sites. Many of us for the rest of our lives will continue to live in old existing communities which have grown casually without over-all design or forethought. That need not prevent us from having some range of choice of environment. Villages and towns are never finished so long as they are populated, and in their growth and flux it is possible to bring them closer to the best they might have been. Sometimes the necessity for revising the old and adding new elements may leave the whole with marked character and individuality, more interesting than though it had been formally planned in the first place. Also, there are numerous towns and villages which, in their setting and in their general design and flavor, have so much of excellence and charm that there should be no thought of losing them. A well-informed sense of values may make it possible to supplement their excellences with other elements which all modern municipalities need, such as adequate provisions for automobiles, in a manner to add to their general quality.

There are, of course, great values in continuity of location if some essential qualities are present. Memories and associations gather around the old home, or the old home town. How fortunate is the family which has a home so favorably placed, so adequate, and so expressive of the family spirit that it can continue through long years as the center of family memories and the place of family reunions. It is the same with the locations of communities. The more wisely and adequately—or fortunately—a community location was determined on, and the better the use made of that location, the less is the probability that it will prove inadequate in the long future.

A careful exploration of the home town may disclose physical elements which might be turned into valuable assets. Perhaps there is a stream running through or near the town. Even if its course is now an unsightly area, covered by weeds or debris, a little imagination and some cooperative effort might turn it into an especially beautiful park or playground. Perhaps a small dam would provide a pond for swimming in summer or skating in winter, or a little study of fish culture might turn it into a fish pond for children. A piece of rough woodland may be transformed into a playground.

There may be an abandoned commercial or industrial building which can be turned to a similar use. We have seen that done in a number of communities. We know of one case where a big, old-fashioned barn was made into a neighborhood center, and two cases where such a barn was turned into a summer theater. Old flour mills have been similarly used. Stone quarries have been made into swimming pools and skating centers. Many towns have idle resources which are waiting to be made into community assets.

I am constantly impressed by the possibilities of beauty and other values which are lying unnoticed and unused, or are being permanently ruined, in and about existing communities. There is play for a large amount of public-spirited effort in becoming aware of these, getting public possession of them, and realizing their possibilities. Often the ugliest places in town are potentially the most beautiful.

There Will Be New Communities. In many cases the community of the future will be a continuation of that of today, in the same location, with many of the same streets, buildings and utilities. But also in the natural course of events new communities will be created. A discussion of the physical setting of the community of the future should have both these prospects in view. However, since it will be the new locations and designs that will be influenced most by present and future thinking, it seems appropriate that a considerable part of our attention should be given to them.

In the century ahead of us, if the structure of society does not crumble unexpectedly, communities will be created or relocated both as a result of changes and developments in our economic life, and because of increasing discrimination as to what constitutes desirable environment for living. Groups of like-minded people will promote housing units and small communities in locations that will be within reasonable travel distance of a considerable number of employment opportunities. Taking the prospect as a whole, it is not idle imagining to consider what would be desirable elements of a new or relocated site for living.

What then would be the physical characteristics of a desirable community? Only occasionally has that general question been asked by active men, and then answered out of mature understanding and sensitiveness to human values. Is it possible to make suggestions concerning the physical needs of a good community, which will help town planners to ask themselves pertinent questions?

During past centuries and in older countries men lived in villages and worked in nearby fields, or lived near the shore where boat landings were feasible, or had their village homes adjacent to mine or quarry. Villages originated as the most natural and convenient places for carrying on such necessary activities. Their locations were frankly utilitarian.

Americans, too, have taken for granted the utilitarian settings of their communities, though the particular reasons for their locations sometimes have been different from those of older time. New railroads located towns somewhat arbitrarily at intervals of six to twenty miles along the route; or areas of scattered farms called for towns to supply necessary services.

This custom of having community locations determined by economic considerations or by requirements of military safety has been so nearly imperative through the ages that it has come to control our thinking. That a community might be located deliberately on a site chosen because it is a fit and beautiful setting was not in the general mental picture which prevailed during the settlement of our country.

Bondage to utilitarian considerations is becoming less and less a physical necessity. More and more it is but a lingering servitude of the mind, a vestige of an obsolescent cultural tradition. But to suggest that community location can be largely independent of an industrial plant or other economic activity is foreign to the current mental set, and, except in case of urban commuting, has seemed impractical, or more generally has not been thought of. Deliberate effort may be necessary to free our minds—to stretch them so we can envision the full possibilities of freedom in community location.

The enlarged and strengthened spirit of community will call for more adequate physical expression than it has had in the past. A suitable location is so vital to good living that interest in relocating communities, or in building new ones, should become current.

In the western world, and until the last one or two generations, a dwelling house was looked upon as something permanent. It might be a major part of the family inheritance passed on to the next generation. That feeling is changing, and probably will continue to change. The average man can begin to think of changing his old home for a better one to fulfill the family dream, even at sacrifice of much of the value of the old. Such practice already is not uncommon, just as industries increasingly find it more feasible to build new physical plants than to rehabilitate old ones.

The same possibility exists as to the physical locations and plants of entire communities. When we have made intelligent and adequate specifications for a community setting we may find it less expensive to choose the best possible location and build the entire structure anew than to modernize the old.

The idea of towns built to specifications is not new. During the past century scores of such have been built, usually by industries for housing employees, but sometimes for other reasons. Partly from industrial necessity, but also partly from industrial habit, living facilities usually were given secondary or even lower consideration. Workmen often were looked on primarily as elements of industrial production, and relatively little study was made as to what would constitute desirable environment for satisfactory living. Pullman, Illinois; Gary, Indiana; and Kohler, Wisconsin, are examples of some of the more reputable undertakings. Since they bear their founders' names they must have been looked upon with pride. Their limitations were more from lack of human understanding than from inadequate financial resources. Various mining towns were little more than groups of squalid, unpainted barracks.

We are developing new attitudes toward building materials. It generally has been considered that a substantial, enduring structure should be permanent. That is less and less considered necessary. Men are learning when to use materials to construct "everlasting" monuments, when to use them for short-term present ends, and even more interestingly, how to use them for what may be either permanent or temporary as interest may dictate. I recall how impressed I was, about forty years ago, to see one of the master construction men of America use massive structures of reinforced concrete for very temporary purposes. Since this man's need was for rugged strength, he built strength; what he built might have lasted for a century. But he needed it for only a year, and when its use was past it was at once removed. He was master of his materials.

We need to think of entire communities in the same way. So long as their physical settings and their plants continue to be reasonably good media for expressing the spirits and aspirations of the members they should be kept. When they essentially fail to do that it may be well to shed them as a snake sheds its skin.

It is not out of disregard for community associations and family memories that we suggest the relocation of inadequately situated communities, but rather the contrary. Some places where we have lived our children would like to forget. There is another place which they think of as home, as the place of good memories; and the physical setting is an important factor in that relationship. It is somewhat within men's power to determine for the future that as memories accumulate around the old home setting there will not need to be a conflict of spirit as to whether to continue to treat it as home because of the old associations, or to leave it and forget it because of the mediocrity or unloveliness of the environment. Memories of the future will be no less important than those of the past; and it is the memories of the future that are partly under our control. It is for those that we can provide memorable settings.

Today, we are informed, about a third of the American population moves each year. That means personal and family rootlessness. Such movement is very different from that of the old-time nomads, who might keep the community structure intact century after century, though moving frequently as a community to maintain the food supply. Sometimes such migration was rhythmic, back and forth between summer and winter pasture; sometimes it was continuous. In America the Miami Indians, as growing population led to exhaustion of the game supply, moved gradually over the country from Florida to Lake Erie. However, in that process they were always the tightly knit, continuing communities.

To some extent present-day migration is due to defect of personality, a vain searching, by change of outward circumstance, for the harmony which can come only by achievement of inner character. Sometimes it is a vain, half-conscious search for desirable living conditions. If they should be found, migration of the family would cease. Very often, of course, one must go to where his work is. Whatever its causes may be, modern nomadism tends to be destructive of community. It is chiefly that part of the population which puts down its roots in relatively permanent residence which keeps alive the best elements of the cultural inheritance.

Community must have beginnings as well as continuity. The immemorial custom of breaking away from the parent community and starting a new one has been a natural and essential part of human existence. America was not settled by nomads, but by people looking for opportunity to put down roots. Where the old is substantially inadequate, then to create anew is natural.

The Location of New Communities. Modern technology and convenience of travel are freeing men from the necessity of living in immediate proximity to their work. Even today, many a man, having taken a job in some industry or institution, may decide to make his home as much as twenty miles away from his work. Conversely, if the nature of an industry definitely fixes its location, it still may be possible for the community in which its employees will live to be located almost anywhere within a considerable area. For instance, if the dominant occupation should be quarrying, it no longer is necessary for the employees to live within a mile or two of the quarry. If we assume that 15 miles is not too far for a man to go to work, then within 15 miles of the job there would be an area of 700 square miles within which to select a desirable community site. If ideas are fairly clear as to what would be the best characteristics of a community location, why not select the most appropriate tract in the entire area? Except in unvarying flat plains, an area of that size probably would include one or several largely unoccupied locations which by natural setting and human art would be highly satisfactory for living.

In case economic requirements fix the location of a town or village in a region devoid of many desirable elements of a living site, as where a railroad junction point on our vast, flat, western plain requires the existence of a town to serve it, or a farming area in a great expanse of flat country calls for a town to serve the locality; it still may not be necessary to accept a fate of monotonous flatness. In several parts of our country the strip mining of coal tears up the country, leaving it quite changed, and sometimes largely destroyed. The same general types of earth-moving equipment are available for changing the appearance of the physical environment of the community where water is available by producing lakes, hills, parks, wooded areas, playgrounds and little wilderness tracts, so that the people, and especially the children, may have an environment of variety and beauty, with some degree of wild nature.

An increasing number of industrial processes are becoming free from requirements as to specific locations. Many of them could operate almost anywhere in the United States. Some of our great corporations have industrial units distributed well over the country, quite regardless of nearby markets or raw materials. In many cases the placing of industries and of communities may be determined by the quality of the locality from a human standpoint. Such elements as climate, health conditions, beauty of surroundings, access to wild country, the presence of lakes, mountains, etc., may be factors in deciding locations. I repeat, the taking into account of such possibilities may be prevented less by economic considerations than by a set of mind from which it is difficult to escape.

Space for the New Community. In determining its physical location the community of the future, let us hope, will give greater weight to other than economic considerations. One of these concerns should be for adequate living space in both quantity and quality. People crave space. When a man has achieved marked economic success one of the commonest ways for him to seek the satisfactions he craves is to acquire an estate where he can have undisturbed space around him. This has been true in nearly all parts of the world from the times of the ancient East Indian and Roman men of wealth and power down to the successful American industrialist today. Walking through the vast groves, gardens and avenues of ancient Hadrian's villa in the beautiful open country east of Rome, one sees an expression of the same urge which moved an American agricultural machinery magnate of the last generation to create a spacious estate in Florida. When a man finds himself in position to realize his dream of what is a good life, provision for ample space is one of the commonest expressions. What the "successful" man achieves is what most men would have if they could.

In the community of the future it will not be possible for each family to have the private ownership of liberal space, with woods and fields and streams; but for a community as a whole to have such a setting is not an unreasonable hope. Quite probably the satisfaction of each individual may be as great (if we omit from consideration the satisfaction of sheer exercise of power) and the inconveniences of ownership much less, than though he had sole ownership. The acquisition of such tracts is more commonly possible because often the terrain which has greatest recreational and esthetic possibilities may be mediocre or even worthless for agriculture, and may not be needed as a town dumping ground, which would have precedence in the minds of many practical persons.

The very idea of such community achievement is partly inhibited by vestiges of class discrimination. I recall visiting the exquisitely furnished palatial home of a wealthy family in Zurich many years ago and listening to a severe criticism of a public housing development. Trying to get at the gist of the criticism, I asked whether the project had experienced irregular financial management or incompetent direction. I was told that there was no such criticism, that the work had been honestly, skillfully and economically handled. The heart of the complaint, I found, was that these workmen's houses contained *bathrooms*. A workman's house with a bathroom! How contrary to the aristocratic sense of social fitness! It may similarly be a vestige of an earlier pattern of thought which would see it as fantastic that the average community of the future should have an ample and beautiful physical setting. If it is not provided, the failure will be due more often to limitation of thought pattern than to inadequacy of financial resources.

Society and Solitude in the Community of the Future. The physical setting of the community of the future should provide both for society and for solitude. W. R. Alger wrote in his *Genius of Solitude:*[20]

> Man is both a gregarious and a solitary animal, as much made for society as for solitude, and as much for solitude as for society. His true life, in a healthy state, is an alternation from one to the other in due proportion. . . . There is something wrong with him whose lonely interviews with nature make him dislike to meet men; something wrong with him whose associations with men unfit him to enjoy retirement. The one should send him to the other with renewed relish.

How many a boy or girl, with a craving to get below the surface of things and to work out meaning for his life, is coerced by the social environment into doing what everyone is doing; how many a man, with potential capacity for great contribution to his times, has been so crowded with associations, busyness and the pressure of trivialities, that finally his spirit was smothered and he gave up the struggle to be his best self! How many of us live in limbo, afraid of the society of real human fellowship and communication, and also afraid of solitude. We communicate often but superficially, and are afraid of exposing our real selves; yet are afraid to meet our own real selves alone.

That is one reason why American life is so deeply committed to mediocrity. It is not because Americans lack capacity for high quality, but because our social habits discourage it. We are friendly to talent, but not to deeper quality. We welcome Billy Graham, Norman Vincent Peale, or Father Sheean, but John the Baptist would be in very bad form, and where would there be a nearby desert for him to go to ?

The banalities of the high school social program, or of the town luncheon club, or of the church society, or of the cocktail party, or of most other social life in the small or large town, may in fact impose a more rigid servitude than would great poverty. The tyranny of youthful opinion can be extreme. Today in very many high schools, quite largely due to mass education following school consolidation, there is strong intolerance of scholarship and of interest in ideas.

We fail both in community and in individual personality. The ancient village was the place where the people did almost the whole of their living—personal, social, economic, religious, educational and esthetic—in intimate relations and in full view of each other. Yet, as in the ancient villages of Britain and of Europe, one had only to step to the edge of the village to be in the "waste" or wild forest and to be alone. Our present intense desire to have partitions between us is due in part to lack of the quality of community, and in part to a feeling that we have no other escape from human contact.

I recall, when an office building in which I was to work was under construction, how shocked I was to find that my office and all the others were to have only clear glass partitions between them. Sound was eliminated, but we all could see each other. How could I endure that lack of separateness and of privacy? As I used that office year after year I found that there was nothing I needed to hide from other people. To see them through the partitions added a social touch, while light from all sides was a distinct advantage. Many of the partitions we build between ourselves and other people are needless. The intuitions we have that we need them do not serve us well.

Yet we also need solitude. Mediocrity is at home in the crowd. The discriminating mind and spirit make their best growths when they have opportunities for periods of quiet and solitude. One reason for the slow rate of human progress is that very often the kind of quality which is encouraged to develop is that which is fortunately situated, or is tough, self-seeking or aggressive. Caesar, Napoleon or Hitler, obsessed by craving for power, may push the way through the crowd to dominance. Men who most extend the range of human insight and depth of feeling nearly always do much of their growing where they are sometimes free from constant contacts with people and with current interests. Most of them have been lonesome men. This was true of Buddha, Jesus, Lucretius, Dante, Descartes, Milton, Shelley, Wordsworth, Spinoza, Channing, Emerson, Thoreau, Lincoln and many others. What is true of great men is true of many of lesser mold but of sure value.

For many such men time to be alone and to renew one's spirits is scarcely less necessary than time for sleep and physical refreshment. If we deprive such persons of opportunity for solitude, the damage to their spirits may be as great as would be the harm to their bodies if we should permanently deny them chance to sleep.

How many such persons would there be? We do not know. Quite frequently marked individuality, unless it is aggressive and thick-skinned, surrenders to the prevailing temper of society, or becomes a disturbed and psychotic personality. Emerson wrote, "To go into solitude a man needs to retire as much from his chamber as from society." Opportunity to sometimes be alone under conditions of quiet natural beauty in many cases would be a refreshing and healing resource, and might come to be used by more persons than we should expect. We have observed that the use of such resources grows through the years.

Love of Nature in the Community of the Future. In every age and every land men have been impelled to add beauty to what was necessary in arts and crafts, and to express their creative spirits even when no utility was involved. Some of their works remain with us as great treasures, partly because their beauty gives us joy, partly because we get hints of the imagination and skills involved, and partly because we are told by the specialists that they have value.

Love of beauty and "art appreciation" are far from being the same. As practiced and experienced, art appreciation combines love of beauty with various other elements, particularly with appreciation of the skill required of the artist. We admire the artist's skill in securing his effects somewhat as we admire a surgeon for his "beautiful" operation in taking out a man's kidney, though the sheer optical effect of his work would not have been pleasing, except to a qualified surgeon.

No small part of art appreciation consists in acquiring merit by owning what others would like to own, or learning the canons of art, which must be important because so many people take them to be so. As with the king who rode naked through the streets wearing invisible clothes which no one but "honest" people could see, and with no one daring to admit seeing him naked, so it is with much art appreciation. If patrons and students of art should be limited to those who take spontaneous joy in it, their ranks would not be crowded.

As to love of nature, such selection has, in fact, been made. It has almost no propaganda, and its possession does not insure prestige. We see the misty light in the oak trees as the young leaves start to come out in the spring, the curve of the woodland brook, the distribution of space and branches in the spreading sycamore tree in winter, the perfect vista down the valley. These move us deeply, not because of the skill of doing them, but for what they are. No art appreciation tells us how to enjoy them, for no authentic textbook of instructions has been prepared. No art connoisseur tells us how much to pay for them, and no art specialist has made chemical tests to find out whether they are genuine, worth a king's ransom, or are imitations and scarcely worth a song. Since many people value what they have been told to value, and since beauty of nature has little or no promotion, it has not the vogue of human art.

Yet for persons sensitive to the qualities of unspoiled nature, natural beauty is a source of gladness, of deep satisfaction, of peace of mind, and of re-creation of mind and body which has few equals in human experience. Though sometimes the beauty is so piercing that it hurts, yet the general effect is of relaxation, peace, harmony. One experiences renewal of his spirit.

The only case I know where love of nature is a dominant cultural trait, grown into the very life and language, is that of Finland. The Finnish Kalevala, a group of folk songs collected and arranged in what has become the great national epic, breathes throughout a strong sense of the beauty of wood and water, of summer green and winter snow. Whereas the English language has perhaps a dozen words for light, the Finnish language has perhaps ten times as many: such as a word for the glint of light on the stream at sunset, the light which shines through the fog on a cool morning, the crisp light on the winter snow—all expressing a sensitiveness to qualities which stir the spirit. Is it beyond imagination that the average American community should have in its surroundings areas which would invite its people to similar appreciation?

Natural beauty is not rare or hard to find. No monopoly can get a corner on it. In my much traveling over rural America during more than half a century I have come across strong love of nature in the most unexpected places. Repeatedly my rural host, usually a farmer, has said to me, "Now, tell me truly, don't you think that this is the most beautiful location for a home that you have ever seen?" From occasionally being asked such a question I came to have a ready and honest answer. I would reply, "I never have seen a more beautiful location for a home." It was an honest answer, for in the almost infinite variety of our country in natural beauty, in the never-ending changes of light and season for each setting, and in endless variety of taste for kinds of beauty, the types and instances are quite uncomparable, and so it is impossible as to a vast number of spots to say that one is more beautiful than any other.

If good advantage is taken of possibilities, the unending diversity of natural settings can give limitless variety and charm to many community environs. Many an American town makes expenditures for "art" and "beautification" far greater than commonly would be necessary to secure a considerable measure of natural beauty in its environs. The most successful treatment of intimate natural landscape that I have seen in all Europe was not any of the famous formal gardens, but a bit of rough country near the west tip of Portugal, at Sintra. Here some rocky hills, such as one might find in any of a thousand localities in America, were grown to woods and supplied with paths so skillfully placed that, even when they were but one or two hundred feet apart, they seemed to be alone in a primeval forest. The paths, seemingly by accident, passed beautiful vistas; and, seemingly by accident, there would be a stone seat just where the vista could be enjoyed. The poet Byron referred to this as "Sintra's glorious Eden." On parts of this tract there were ruins of old Moorish forts which added interest, and a summer castle of the former king; yet the beauty was in the treatment of the woods and hills in a way that entailed relatively little construction or maintenance cost. What is needed in many parts of America is not primarily large expense, but an active sense of natural beauty.

The Need for Bits of Nature about the New Community. If a great man has been a native of a town, and especially if he has lived his life there, his fellow townsmen may honor him and perhaps maintain his home as a shrine. In contrast, the community of the future will give its chief attention, not to the important persons who were born or lived there in the past, but to those who might be born there in the future. It will honor them, not by stone monuments, but by providing an environment in which their full possibilities may be realized, so far as that is within the power of the community.

The chief measure of a great community will not be that it has fine public buildings and a strong economic base, or that its churches are full. All these may be present and highly desirable, yet unless they are infused with reverence for quality, both that of the past and what might come, those other characteristics may only weld more tightly the chains of mediocrity.

I am told that in many a Swiss village, while there is faithful, loving care for all children at home and in school, there is also constant watch for the boy or girl of unusual promise, for persons who may bring to the home community, and perhaps to the larger world, clearer insight and wider vision. "Without vision the people perish." What is more important to a town than to be sensitive to the person of potential vision who might be born there, and to give him opportunity to fulfill his promise—not primarily for his own advantage or for the prestige of the town, but so that his or her possibilities shall not be lost to society?

So it must be in the community of the future. The village library should not just satisfy the prevailing taste; it should be a treasury of intellectual and spiritual and literary wealth, waiting for the occasional person who will crave and use this wealth. Just as many a home of generations past kept a room that might seldom be used, but which was always ready for

the honored guest; so will the community of the future be sensitive and ready for the exceptional guest that may come to it
by birth, or by the arrival of new families to live in the community. And when that course is taken there may be an unexpected and surprising result. It may turn out that a much
greater proportion of the children of the community than were
expected will be found taking advantage of those opportunities.
Greatness is partly inborn, but partly it rises in response to
expectation and belief in its coming.

These comments have a bearing on what should be the
physical setting of the community of the future. That community should try to provide, as part of its physical property
and its environs, wild lands, little wildernesses, natural
woods and other resources, where thoughtful people can find
relief from constant social pressure and can recover whole-
ness of personality. Such tracts will have various uses. Young
children will like to explore them and will get first-hand contact with nature. Freedom at times from the regimentation
which modern life, especially school, imposes, is necessary
for their relaxation and full development. Parts of such tracts
will furnish opportunities for family or other small group recreation; and many a person will find there a place where he
can steal away for a short time to live with himself in an in-
spiring setting.

Nature conditions are changing in America. What once was
free must now be recovered by design. Two centuries ago in
America one could drink safely from almost any stream. Today, despite millions spent to reduce pollution, it is a risk to
drink from almost any. "The old swimming hole" existed near
almost any village. Now its use is proscribed by the State
Board of Health. Today chance for solitude with nature is far
gone, and will be largely lost, despite the widespread possibilities, unless we make specific provisions for its preservation. We have not adjusted our minds to that change. For the
everyday life of childhood, where access to nature is most
necessary, the problem lies largely with the community, or
very commonly with two or more communities working in uni-
son. With clear purpose the problem generally can be solved.

Can we not look forward to the time when each community,
as an accepted part of its resources, will have at least sev-

eral hundred acres of play ground, family recreation space, and true wilderness ? "Man does not live by bread alone," and should set aside a part of the land for cultivation of the spirit.

The Technology of the Community of the Future. The animals of Alaska have learned to endure cold. Those of the lower Amazon have become largely immune to tropical parasites and disease. If each should be put in the place of the other, both would die. Creatures become able to endure what they have long experienced. It is under new conditions that they fail to survive.

Men have evolved gradually in a world of danger, hardship and general insecurity, and have learned to survive in that world. A world of security, comfort and abundance is new to them, and they have not yet become immune to its dangers. Rome deteriorated in its time of wealth and power, and so have many other cultures.

Today our country seems to be entering on a period of internal security from poverty, to a time when most men can be assured of a considerable margin above their imperative needs. If we survive under that new condition we shall be one of the few cultures ever to do so. Our first attention may well be to developing the newly needed immunity to the spiritual diseases of prosperity, as even more important than the securing of economic abundance. Unless we can master dishonesty and narrow self-interest in dealing with each other, and unless we can discipline our bodies to be free from drugs, narcotics and opiates, and can keep ourselves fit in body and mind and our spirits free from jealousy, indulgence and passion for power, the economic abundance we secure may be only a prelude to social and personal disintegration. The Biblical parable has long-time significance: "The land of a rich man brought forth plentifully; and he thought to himself, 'What shall I do, for I have nowhere to store my crops?' And he said, 'I will do this: I will pull down my barns, and build larger ones; and there will I store all my grain and my goods. And I will say to my soul, Soul, you have ample goods laid up for many years; take your ease; eat, drink, be merry.' But God said to him, 'Fool! This night your soul will be required of you.'"

If we can assume the qualities which will sustain and survive economic abundance, we can look forward to technical
developments for the community of the future which will make
the best of present communities seem primitive. With a world
at peace, and with the new habit of industrial research push-
ing back the frontiers of knowledge and reducing the amount
of effort for any given amount of production, vast undertakings
will be necessary to make full use of our productive capacity.
The community of the future can design the most adequate
physical setting and plant, with reasonable prospect of achieving them.

It should be possible, for instance, to put an entire community under a high roof, with heating, cooling and air treatment for the whole. All air entering the enclosure could be
filtered of dust and pollen, corrected as to its ionic characteristics, and given the temperature and humidity of a spring
morning in the mountains. Outgoing air would carry with it
waste gases and much of the dust. The householder may scan
the goods in the store by television, and have them delivered
by pneumatic tube. Such developments would be less improbable and fanciful than some which already have taken place in
other fields.

One reason for risking such a fanciful picture is to emphasize the fact that there would be small reason to try at
present to plan in detail the physical design of the community
of the future. Technical development moves at a steadily accelerated pace. So far as the physical mechanics of community are concerned, we may do well in some respects to plan
ahead for one or two generations at a time. During the past
century in New York City many beautiful, sometimes palatial,
homes have been built, designed by master architects and
constructed to last a thousand years, only to be torn down in
a few years to make way for city growth.

Perhaps we need a new concept for building. Instead of
constructing homes, stores, churches and other edifices by
traditional standards as though we were creating monuments
for centuries to come, it might be better to think of our houses
as we think of our clothes, as serving us until we need or desire change. A man and wife at first need a home for two.
Ten years later, with a house full of young children, they need

a home for childhood. Ten years later adolescents are entertaining their friends, and a quite different home is appropriate. In another ten or twenty years, as grandparents of the family, the two are again alone, and find much space a burden. How frequently do we see elderly people living alone in large, nearly empty houses. Why not, at appropriate times, take away the unsuitably constructed house, or the surplus or inappropriate parts of it, and bring another? Some of the furniture within, and the grounds without, would remain to be bearers of associations and precious memories.

Such a change of policy concerning housing would not require any fundamentally new inventions or discoveries, but chiefly a change of mental attitude. Perhaps the flexibility of living which would result might be conducive to the flexibility of mind which is needed by the world of today, and will be even more needed by the world of tomorrow.

The idea we would give our readers concerning the physical structure of the community of the future is not a set of rules to build by, but an attitude to think by. Discussions of widths of streets, areas of school grounds, or provisions of zoning ordinances, should be with specialists in those fields, or at least with the particular case in view. One general point we would emphasize. In planning the community of the future it is well to break free from servitude to conventional patterns and to think through the problems to reasonable conclusions.

For instance, in the process of drafting zoning ordinances, our traditions date from a time when factories were ugly things, to be removed as fully as possible from residence environments. Today *in some instances,* a factory may be as attractive as a church, and may give the neighborhood boys and girls some additional picture of the processes by which men live.

As to its physical setting, the community of the future may fulfill human needs, and may give expression to the spirit of men, to a far greater degree than has the community of the past. In the community of the future tradition should be a source of judgment and inspiration, but not the determining control. The spirit of men calls for a more ample setting than generally has been achieved. Modern technology can help to provide it.

Incentives to Good Community Planning. More and more frequently the physical plants for entire towns or subdivisions are being constructed at one time, the designs being provided by professional town planners. These are promoted by industrialists, contractors, town planners and others. How can influence be brought to bear on these agencies so that their planning and building will be done with the welfare of the entire community in view, and without omitting consideration of any major community interest? Of course, there is no simple answer to that question, but there are ways in which average individuals can powerfully affect the course of community planning and construction.

As we come to make our choices of where to live and work, our mental images of what it is we seek will be constant factors in our search. If we have no clear pictures and no well-defined ideas we will be very subject to salesmanship. Insofar as that is the situation, the industrialist, the planner and the man who makes a business of building need not think further than of cost and profits, depending on forceful salesmanship to find purchasers of what they build. Doubtless some eye-catching devices would be added to house or land to help the salesman.

If there should be general distribution of appreciation of what is important in the physical setting of a community, those who plan and build would soon take that fact into consideration. If buyers or renters show intelligent, well-informed discrimination in searching for homes and for suitable community settings, builders and planners will soon become sensitive to what is wanted. The well-planned and well-built community will sell more readily. Also, as people constantly move about hunting for desirable places to live they educate themselves. A single well-planned and well-built town or subdivision, in which the major factors of good physical setting have been provided, will create demand for others.

Thus, the emergence of adequate, fine community settings need not be forever deferred. In view of the present mobility of the American population, and the constant search for work and community that may be permanent and satisfactory, informed choice on the part of families seeking places to live can be a powerful educational influence. To a considerable extent the physical setting and plant of the community of the future will be what people want and search for. As wants become more intelligently discriminating, the quality of the physical setting of the community will improve.

Town Planning. We have drawn attention to some of the physical characteristics of a good community which are most apt to be overlooked. Some other elements are so evident that no more than mention of them is necessary. Such factors as climate, topography, economic assets, natural beauty of the region, transportation facilities, are generally in mind. Other factors are convenient access to population centers, good water supply, good drainage, good soil, good health conditions, fuel and energy supply (such as availability of gas), freedom from danger of being overrun by metropolitan growth, small probability of natural disaster such as flood, freedom from danger of being swamped by some large industrial development, such as harbor development on a water front.

Some elements of town planning are so prominently in the minds of town planners that there is scarcely any necessity for mentioning them. Such factors include widths of streets, absence of heavy through traffic in residence units, zoning policy, parks and playgrounds, school locations, size of building lots, provisions for automobile parking, convenience of markets, churches, schools, etc., control of smoke and other air pollution, and noise.

There are other factors of planning that are gradually working their way into American thinking. Among these are neighborhood units for larger communities, the limitation of size of towns by the help of "green belts," and the prevention of "ribbon towns," which latter has actually been promoted as the ideal by a prominent rural sociologist.

It is beyond the range of this discussion to enter into the details of the planning of community townsites.

X

Local Government
in the Community of the Future

In such a discussion as this of the community of the future, any effort to outline in detail the structure and functions of local government would be out of place. We shall try only to point out some of the general attitudes, aims and considerations which tend to influence its character. Except where methods of government are unfortunately regimented and rigid, the particular methods which can best be used will vary with time and circumstance.

We have said that for a community to regain life and vigor it must have necessary functions. This is true in government as elsewhere. It is a generally sound principle that government is best when its administration is as nearly as possible in the hands of those most immediately involved. That is particularly true as to the community. The people of a good community know their circumstances as no one else does. They can best take the action which fits the circumstances, and can avoid the arbitrariness, bureaucracy and regimentation which tend to result from government at a distance. One of the strongest impulses or principles of human communities the world over is that the community should be allowed to handle its own affairs and relationships, and to solve its own community problems, in its own way, without outside interference.

Yet there is no principle of human relations which is absolute and supreme. Every such principle is conditioned and modified by others, and good government lies in achieving a proper relation among them. For instance, in America the principle of local freedom of action and home rule is subject to the American doctrine of the equal right of all men to self-respect, dignity, and opportunity. We see this interaction of principles in the issue of race discrimination and segregation.

Some sections of the country would erect the principle of local self-determination—states' rights or home rule—into the controlling principle of government. Others see the "universal" principles of human rights and human dignity as controlling over all others. Thus two principles of action, both of them sound, come into conflict. There are numerous such actual dilemmas in human affairs. In the absence of good will there is no way of solving such dilemmas except through some form of force.

But it is not only the principle of universal human rights which limits local management of local affairs. There are various elements of local government in which efficient administration is possible only on a large scale, entirely beyond the range of local government. The administration of the post office is such a case, though it might be possible for local communities to have more responsibility for the administration of local offices.

Other areas where it is not feasible for the locality to administer its own affairs are: rules for operating railway traffic through the town, automobile speed through the community, precautions against contagious diseases, the administration of social security (since people are constantly moving about), the right of childhood to be free from economic exploitation, the disposal of sewage and the control of stream pollution where it would affect other communities. There are various twilight zones between areas where home rule should be fully recognized and those where "universal" rights or long-range expediency or convenience should rule. The public mind and spirit are constantly trying to resolve these marginal cases by good will and understanding, or by strategy and through various expressions of power.

Good Will in the Community Government of the Future. By far the best solvent for the conflicts of contrasting "principles" or interests in the small community is good will. So far as the adjustment of seemingly conflicting human rights and responsibilities is concerned, the power of formal government need come into play only where good will fails.

The family and the small, face-to-face community are the birthplaces of good will. Normally there is more of it within the family than in the community, more of it in the community than in the state or nation, and more of it within the nation than between nations. One value of local community government is that it is a training ground for the growth of good will. "Peace on earth" will come, not primarily because of treaties or world governments, but because the quality of good will has had such vigorous growth in the more intimate relationships that it has become a way of life which overflows its bounds and gives character to human relations on a larger scale.

There is an old American saying, "Eternal vigilance is the price of liberty." That is true to the extent that good will is absent. Does a child exercise vigilance against its parents? Where a man and wife are vigilant against each other, the prospects for family well-being are not good. So in the community. In many a good community it would be considered a scandal for a man to be so vigilant against his neighbor or any member of the community that he would lock his doors at night.

In a good community the local government itself can be like a good friend or neighbor, more than an instrument of power. In a good community the children will run to meet the policeman; in a poor community they will run away from him. In the village where I live, in the handling of juvenile delinquency the chief of police is friendly adviser and coordinator of the efforts of parents, teachers, ministers and physicians to remove the causes of troublesome stresses. Where punishment of law-breaking is necessary in the community it is a process of discipline and correction, rather than of retaliation. Humiliating publicity is avoided, except where it seems necessary in a process of public education.

What we have said of good will in local government is not a sentimental effusion, but a statement of what can be and is the social climate in many a small community, and of what should be generally characteristic of the community of the future. This attitude is important, in the interest both of the community and of its members, and for its influence on wider social relationships, which in the end are mostly the projection of the spirit of community or the result of its absence.

Decision by Consensus.   In the ancient community, voting as we know it was largely unknown. As voting emerged it was looked on as a refined form of conflict, sometimes as alternative to war. Over most of the world the very ancient community had a fairly well defined method of resolving issues and determining the responsibility for crimes or misdemeanors. The village elders grew into their places by general recognition of their weight of personality and judgment, or by tradition, as when the eldest in each family was considered qualified. When an issue was to be considered the elders would meet, in good weather sitting in a circle of stone seats around the village tree. The other villagers would gather around in a larger circle. As the issue would be discussed, most of the talking would be by the elders, though any person in the village might express an opinion, or offer evidence. This process would continue, in very important cases at intervals for perhaps weeks or months, until the matter was so thoroughly threshed out that there was but one opinion in the village. So long as there was marked division the matter was considered undecided. In case of trial for crime or misdemeanor it was the general result that by the time the hearing was concluded there remained no doubt as to the facts, and the accused, if guilty, had confessed his guilt. This process sometimes was time-consuming, but the absence of remaining rancor, resentment and other stresses was a very great social asset.

This practice of decision by consensus has existed in the Society of Friends (the Quakers) for more than three hundred years. I believe that the "London Yearly Meeting of Friends" has conducted its business for that length of time without taking a vote. It is far from being an obsolete practice. In many boards of directors, often of important organizations, a division by vote is a rare occurrence. Important matters commonly are discussed until there is substantial unanimity. Where there is general agreement it is customary for the one or few with divergent opinions to defer informally to the group. However, if a single respected member has a strong feeling of divergence the matter may be carried over until the division of opinion has been resolved. Perhaps a lone member has sound reason for his position, and may change the opinion of the others.

A man who was for long years member of the Oxford, England, City Council, and at one time mayor of the city, stated it to be his observation that whenever there was a nearly equal division in a vote, it was strong evidence that the decision had been prematurely made, and that further consideration would have been wise. Local community government is the best field for the development of this spirit.

In the village government of Yellow Springs, Ohio—population 3000—this temper prevails at the time this is written. The personnel of the council is greatly varied, with right-wing Republican, left-wing Democrat, negro and white, employer and employee. There is strong independent and uncowed opinion, but a genuine desire to get at the merits of issues, with absence of a habit of dividing into cliques. Where there is marked difference of opinion those differing most may meet privately to explore their differences. In a period of five years of active growth of the village, with many important local issues to decide, there have been only two decisions by other than unanimous vote.

This extended comment on decision by consensus may seem out of place in a discussion of local government in the community of the future. Yet the issue is vital and fundamental. The temper of mind and the social climate which such methods reflect is what makes a good community. They apply not only to government, but to all relationships. Actual peace on earth will be chiefly that spirit grown widespread, or otherwise it will be but an uncertain truce or a new servitude. In a good community, law is for the convenience and effectiveness of administration, rather than for the organization of power.

The Issues of Local Government. Although the spirit of government is primary, yet a good spirit needs good instruments for its expression. Relatively little imagination or creative thinking has been evident in the development of community government in America. The community of the future will have not only a good spirit, but it will evolve adequate methods. Only a hint can be given here of issues which will require consideration.

The community will need a large element of home rule; that is, the right to work out its own policies and methods, rather than have them dictated by state or nation. Of course, this right must always be qualified by the need for central control over matters of a general nature which are beyond or outside the range of local control. What those matters are will depend on times and circumstances. For instance, state control over local sewage disposal should depend on whether it actually concerns larger areas.

One of the worth-while innovations in American local government is the charter commission, whereby the people of a community may work out their own structure of government. Another valuable creation is the council-manager form of municipal government, which in many communities is highly efficient and a great improvement over earlier methods. Another is the elimination of party designations from candidates in local elections. Still other developments are the policy of zoning the parts of a municipality and its environs to prevent inappropriate occupation and use, and the creation of local planning commissions to guide physical development.

Some necessary developments relate to the spirit rather than to the form of local government. For instance, there is needed a spirit of thrift and of social responsibility. Bond issues for local improvements should not burden coming generations with taxes to pay for present use. Real estate developments should not ignore the long-time fitness of the community setting.

One general aim of government should be to eliminate all that is arbitrary or capricious from human relations, and in each case to suit the course to the actual conditions. Since conditions vary endlessly, the closer the government is to the situation, and the more fully it knows the circumstances, then in general the less arbitrary will be its action. For this reason local government usually is better than centralized administration wherever the issues involved are local.

In some states the control of the structure of all municipal governments is in the hands of the state, and every municipal government has the same structure as every other one in its class. In other states municipalities have a wide range of freedom in local government, subject, of course, to uniform respect for recognized human rights and to certain uniformities of law and administration. Within those limits each village, town or city can create its own administrative structure. Such freedom is highly desirable to enable live communities to work out their own policies and programs. One of the weaknesses of France is the enforced uniformity of local government, and the centralization of nearly all local authority in the national capital.

Marked incompetence in local administration cannot count on survival. Unless local communities handle their affairs effectively their functions will be taken over by state or nation. Democracy depends on competence for self-government; competence is learned by actual participation in government, and the best school for participation and for development of competence is the local community where people may know the facts they are dealing with, and can observe the results of their actions and policies. A nation with a broad foundation of competent and reasonable local self-government will have a reservoir of ability which can be drawn upon for services in larger fields, and it will be relatively secure from dictatorships, and from wild fluctuations of policy.

If a community with a considerable element of self-government can free itself from arbitrary bondage to tradition, will act in a spirit of good will and with courage, and will inform itself as to significant experiences of other communities the world over, it can find reasonable solutions for most of its problems. The very independence and resulting diversity of community efforts over the country will provide a laboratory in government, with the result that the elements of uniformity which emerge will not be the fruit of dictation, but from common judgment growing out of experience.

XI

Economic Life
in the Community of the Future

At the east end of Santa Maria Island in the Azores is a great bluff, steep as a house roof, extending from the ocean upwards for many hundreds of feet. Clinging to the foot of the bluff and just out of the reach of ocean storm waves is a village whose inhabitants live by fishing and by raising grapes on narrow terraces on the steep face of the bluff. For a person spending his life in that village there are two major inexorable facts of physical existence—the restless ocean in front and that vast towering rock behind. They make the physical framework of his life. His only chance to escape from that rigid setting is to migrate.

How different his life from that of one who lives in the Mississippi Valley! For the latter, paved roads stretch out beyond the horizon in every direction. Other communities and cities and towns are near by. He lives in a larger world.

There are great differences in the kinds of worlds men live in. Some have range and choice and freedom while others are confined within narrow and unyielding limits. This is true as to one's economic as well as to his physical environment. For cases of narrow, rigid economic limits one might cite a copper mining town in Utah, where most workers, isolated in a small town in a vast desert, have just one possible employer. Almost the only obvious opportunity for choice is to flee the region. In the coal mining towns of Kentucky, Tennessee and West Virginia we find people living in similarly circumscribed economic cages. In many another "company town" the range of choice is not much greater.

Yet in such restricted economic circumstances natural individual interest and aptitudes may vary as greatly as in people living in circumstances of wider economic choice. Where interest and aspiration are denied by the fixed setting of life there tends to be frustration.

In deliberately selecting a physical site for building a good community it is not probable that the choice would be a narrow strip of steeply sloping rock just out of reach of the sea and at the foot of a vast and beetling cliff. Similarly, those who may decide upon the *economic* setting of a good community probably would not select a one-industry town, the industry owned and controlled by strangers hundreds of miles away, with the residents and workers having nothing to say as to program or policy. Even a one-crop agricultural community, committed to cotton or wheat or cattle, may give so little vocational choice as to be a deadening setting for ranging occupational interest. A good community will seek varied economic opportunity, or a setting in which such variety is possible.

Even in adverse settings men seldom are the helpless pawns of fate. Take, for instance, the village between the ocean and the cliff on Santa Maria. The island is a stopping-place for several transcontinental air lines. A little well-placed publicity in America, and the construction of some simple guest houses, probably would bring to that village as many guests as could be accommodated—persons for whom the elemental ruggedness of the setting and the simple hospitality of the villagers would provide an ideal environment for spiritual rest and refreshment. Should a community of interest be desired for guests, invitations might go only to some particular class, such as scholars or artists.

Similarly, some purposeful individuals "condemned" to live in a Utah copper mining town might break the monotony by promoting an open desert camp for eastern boys and girls. An imaginative management might help to find many ways for making life interesting. Where there is opportunity to freely choose the economic environment for a community, it generally is wise to insure a wide range of choice. Where fate has placed us in a narrow setting from which we cannot well escape, then creative imagination generally can add range and quality to the possibilities.

The economic quality of a community depends not only on the choice of employers available, but also on the presence or absence of the spirit of community. A sharecropper in middle Mississippi may have the choice of twenty landlords

for whom to work, or he may become a carpenter or a black-
smith, but regardless of the choice he makes he may find the
same rigid caste system of superior master and inferior serv-
ant. The prevailing fixed social pattern tends to reduce the
variety of economic relationships. So, in some American
economic environments, while there may be considerable range
of firms to work for, they may all have similar qualities, attitudes, and limitations.

What, then, are the qualities to be sought in the economics
of a good community ? A fundamental element is that the entire community is an organic whole, that no part violates and
nullifies the spirit of another part. For instance, it would
mar the quality of a community for it to be a subordinate unit
in a large-scale political tyranny. No matter how wisely local plans should be made, they might be capriciously brushed
aside by the will of the over-all dictator. Wherever any economic element is by necessity on such a large scale that the
community cannot control its own destiny in the matter, then
the control should be by orderly lawful process in which local
interests may be considered and judged impartially.

For instance, a large privately owned "public" utility must
have policies which govern its relations with many municipalities. If one of them considers that it has been unfairly treated
as to rates or quality of service it can appeal to a governmental body, and has a right to an impartial hearing. Action
without regard to legitimate community interest is largely
eliminated.

In the matter of private industry this is not so commonly
the case. A private corporation may close or remove a plant
which is the main economic support of a community, where
the employees have their homes and their social roots, and
they may have no redress. However, such capricious migration of industry is now being challenged.

In a good community there is an attitude of general sharing of opportunity and responsibility. Industries vary greatly
in this respect. Many are closely controlled, with neither
stockholders, employees nor the communities in which they
are located having any determining part in administration or
policy, except as stockholders send in their proxies, or labor
unions threaten to strike. There is no simple remedy for this

condition; we are still far short of knowing how best to combine industrial efficiency and participation of those most directly affected, including the community where an industry is located.

Among the criteria for measuring the quality of a community, then, we should include the extent to which the sources of economic livelihood are integrated into its life. Can the industries by which it lives be picked up and removed without its having any choice in the matter? Are the civic relations of the industry to the community determined by those who share its life, or must such matters be referred to strangers at a distant headquarters? Are industrial policies which directly affect it influenced by the spirit of the community, or are they determined by management in a distant metropolis?

As to large-scale industry, the answers to such questions must come in part from a general increase of considerateness and sensitiveness to local interests on the part of industrial management. There has been such increase, especially on the part of public utilities. However, where there is a choice between relatively small industry on the human scale, or large-scale, relatively impersonal industry, the former, integrated into the local life, has some marked advantages. Its owners and management are part of the community; they share the interests and responsibilities of their neighbors, and the local spirit and atmosphere. The ethical standards of the community tend to become the standards of the business. The attitude of class consciousness and class conflict, with resulting restriction of output on the part of employees, is foreign to the spirit of community, and is less often present.

Small-scale industry has a larger place in our common life than is generally realized. Increase of technology, while it leads to centralization and to automation in some fields, also favors the birth of a vast number of small industries. It is by no means visionary or impracticable to plan for small-scale, indigenous, home-owned industry. Had it been the hope and aim of industrial America to make small industrial units feasible and economical, much greater progress might have been made in that direction. The time is not past for such purpose to have a large degree of fulfillment.

The time probably is past for small-scale society to live in isolation, whether as to economic life, education, or any

other field. The peoples and interests of the world are becoming interdependent. In economic life the feasible alternative to centralized large-scale industry, ruled from the top,
is not small units existing in isolation from each other, but
rather autonomous small units in some way federated for their
mutual benefit. (Industrial cooperation is mentioned further
in the statement on "Suggested Industrial Standards.")

Growth of the spirit of community helps to make interdependence and cooperation the more feasible, without destroying desirable elements of independence. The weakness of the
community spirit in America makes industrial cooperation
more difficult, but not less necessary for the existence and
survival of small industry.

The existence of small-scale community industry should
help rather than hinder the emergence of recognized common
ethical standards for business. Where mutual respect, mutual confidence and a spirit of fair play are in control, similar problems tend to be answered in the same way, not by
compulsion, but by inherent reasonableness. The following is
an effort to suggest the kinds of economic standards which
would emerge where the spirit of community is in control. It
may seem out of place to comment so in detail on business
principles in a discussion of the community of the future. Yet
community life is one, and community cannot thrive if a major
element of its life is conducted by standards foreign to its
spirit. The creation of the community of the future is a great
adventure, which must include economics as well as other
fields.

Suggested Industrial Standards
in a Good Community

1. Freedom for Industry and Freedom in Industry. Every
man craves for himself, and industrialists crave for their industries, as much freedom of action as is compatible with the
welfare of industry and of society as a whole. As to industries
as such, we can conduct them so that they will justify the respect and confidence of employees and of the public, and will
make bureaucratic supervision, regulation, or public seizure
unnecessary and unpopular.

Excessive size of a business nearly always reduces individual freedom of action, and has certain other social disadvantages. More men take orders, and fewer share in policy making. The small business man is constantly tempted or threatened for profit's sake to merge with or sell to large business. When he does so he commonly restricts freedom of action. He should consider small business not only from the profit standpoint, but also from the standpoint of social values. Public and legislative policy may well be considered which will tend to hold business to reasonable limits of size.

The employees of *small* business are also *people*. They crave reasonable freedom of action, and significant interests. Sometimes the small business man who cries loudly for freedom for his enterprise may not recognize the same cravings in his employees. The principle of treating other people as one would fairly want to be treated should apply also in his relations with them. So far as it is actually feasible they should share in policy making and in ownership. So far as they show competence, responsibility and interest they should share with management in the adventure of business.

2. Reasonableness. Good business requires absence of arbitrariness. If a contract through an innocent error has a provision which would work serious hardship, that provision should not be enforced. If conditions of an agreement greatly change, reasonableness will take such changes into account to insure fair play. Contracts and agreements should be considered as records of fair dealing, never as traps to catch a person at a disadvantage. In all economic relations we should exercise that understanding and reasonableness which a fair-minded man would like to receive.

3. A Fair Profit. The expression, "a fair profit," has sometimes been used as a mystery word, both confusing the public about the facts of business, and quieting the conscience of the businessman who may be taking about as much as he can get from society for what he gives. Business income should be reduced to its elements, so that both the public and the businessman himself will understand clearly what he means by a fair profit. The following elements may be recognized as included in the cost of doing business for which compensation is justified and necessary in the public interest.

(a) *Interest on the capital safely invested in the undertaking.* This ought to be only the going rate of interest where good security is offered.

(b) *Compensation for risk and uncertainty.* This can take various forms, such as additional interest on capital or additional capitalization. In some well-established businesses the risk is small. In other ventures, such as promoting an invention in which there is perhaps only one chance in several of success, compensation for risk may need to be several times as much as the total capital invested, in order to make up for the losses on many unsuccessful projects. Many businesses have definite elements of uncertainty, such as possible sudden cessation of demand. However, while compensation for risk and uncertainty in some cases may be very large, it should not be unlimited. When such compensation has been adequately made, further payments on that account should be discontinued. Compensation for risk and uncertainty should not be an excuse for taking great unearned profits for an indefinite period.

(c) *Operating expense.* Included in operating expense, if for convenience we may stretch that term, should be such costs as labor, materials, insurance, taxes, depreciation, selling, advertising, maintenance, pension and retirement funds, and incidentals. Operating expenses often include many items the public is not aware of. Often an industrialist fails because he himself has overlooked unavoidable elements of expense. On the other hand, operating expenses should not be used as a way to pay hidden profits.

(d) *Obsolescence.* Most businesses become obsolete in time. Since human judgment is uncertain it often is wise to take enough profit to retire the capital investment within a reasonably short time. Sometimes a product can expect to hold a market for but a brief period, and then the obsolescence charge should be high. The boy selling smoked glasses for looking at an eclipse needs to retire his capital investment in thirty minutes, whereas a well-built and well-located apartment building may have a dependable life of fifty years or more.

On the other hand, when the investment in an enterprise has been paid back by obsolescence charges it should not continue to be the basis for further profits. Prices for the product or the service should go down, or the product or service should be improved, or wages should go up, or the income should be used in the public service, so that the owner is no longer taking profits on an investment that already has been returned to him.

(e) *Management*. The management of a business deserves compensation. Management often has responsibility and indirect expenses and wear and tear that other employees or the general public seldom guess. Such burdens justify a scale of compensation for management on a higher level than that of a salaried employee who does not have that responsibility. However, such needs do not justify management setting itself apart on a high income level which makes the manager into a person of privilege. Economic privilege has followed feudal privilege and has maintained the concept of superior classes. The industrial manager sometimes thinks of himself as having won his way into a privileged class with the right of exploiting society. He feels that he must keep up with a privileged class of Joneses. The manager should get no more as manager than his abilities would command in the open market. It is doubtful whether the quality of management services in America is improved by paying annual salaries, as of 1956, in excess of perhaps $50,000, after taxes, and plus reasonable business expense accounts. Higher income may enable a man to live as a member of a favored social class, but may not improve the quality of his work.

(f) *Compensation for the entrepreneur*. A man who stakes his life prospect on building a business deserves some compensation during years of prosperity for the long, lean years when he went without economic satisfactions and poured his time, life and resources into a difficult prospect. But here, again, such compensation should not be unlimited. An upper limit of compensation as entrepreneur might be the amount of the more adequate income he relinquished during the years, with interest, and compensation for the time and energy he used over what would have been required in a position without such risk and responsibility, plus compensation for risk, as previously mentioned. Here, too, even generous compensation for such work may soon come to a limit, and the position of entrepreneur should not be the basis for indefinite and unlimited profits.

(g) Reserves for contingencies. In order to meet unexpected contingencies, to provide resources for growth, and to be protected against the ups and downs of business conditions, reserves are needed, by whatever name they may be called. These should be controlled and administered by the business, but if such legitimate charges on the business as those already mentioned have been adequately met, these reserves, whether or not they are invested in the business, should not be the basis for larger profits to the investors in the business. They morally belong to the public.

(h) Trusteeship funds. The moral ownership by the public of earnings beyond what are necessary to meet all legitimate costs such as those mentioned rests on a solid basis. No man, and no business, creates wealth by itself. Each generation inherits the wisdom, experience and accumulated wealth of the past. The public order in which business may be conducted, the general level of education without which business could not be carried on, the quality of community which provides a good social climate, the development of moral standards that sustain business, the inventions and discoveries, the skills, the administrative methods, the inheritance of freedom and justice—all these are handed on from the past and constitute the setting in which business is possible. There are no self-made men. All men are made largely by the social inheritance of today and of earlier generations.

A good business will strive constantly to reduce its legitimate costs and to serve the public by low prices, high quality, and good service, and by adequate wages and good working conditions. Sometimes an enterprise finds itself making more money than is necessary to meet all the costs we have mentioned. It may be paying top wages, and higher wages might be creating a privileged class of the particular workmen who happen to be employed in that particular business, but who may be no more deserving than other employees in businesses that would not survive if they should pay nearly as much. It may be that prices for the company's product already are low, and that lower prices would be a hardship on the industry as a whole. Yet earnings may keep mounting.

What shall be done with those profits? They should be used for the public good. From practical experience we may believe that such funds, often or usually, will be used more wisely if administered by business ownership and management than if taken by the government for taxes or paid out in exorbitant wages; but by some method they should be returned to society. The owners or managers of the business should act as trustees for such accumulated earnings. They should be considered no more the property of the business than the funds they might administer as trustees of a non-profit hospital. They might be used for noncommercial research, perhaps in fields that suffer for lack of prospect for economic returns; or for education; or for preservation of public resources of beauty which the public has not yet come to appreciate. In general they can be used to give a chance for those values to be born which are in need of social midwives. Today a large amount of such excess earnings are taken out as private profits. None of them should be so taken.

Thus we see that this mysterious expression, "a fair profit," unless it is reduced to its elements, can be used to confuse a situation so that those who have title to a business can take out of it as much as the traffic will bear, and yet feel innocent. Only when we have broken down business income into its elements can we see what are the legitimate charges on business, and when they are adequately met. In that process the mystery expression, "a fair profit," might disappear.

4. *Business Must Pay.* Honest private business which is not subsidized must pay its way or fail. It must meet such charges against it as those described above, or do injustice somewhere. In an industry conducted in accord with sound social and economic standards, profits are the best measure of competence. The necessity of business to pay its way is a great moral and prophylactic force for efficiency, economy, and productiveness. It gives honest private industry its great merit over politically managed public business where inefficiency, wastefulness, poor judgment and real failure may be hidden by subsidy and taxation. (Many local public services, such as municipal water supplies, are honestly, efficiently and non-politically managed, and so are not subject to this criticism.) Any private business conditions, such as arbitrary monopoly, special privilege, or appropriation of natural resources without paying for them, which make it less neces-

sary for business to exercise thrift, efficiency and competence, are contrary to the public interest.

5. *Open Records.* The very foundation of business is mutual confidence. Few other qualities are so conducive to economy and stability. Mutual confidence without a full sharing of
information, or at least willingness to share it, sometimes
does exist, but its continuance is precarious. Openness and
confidence tend to go together. The public cannot know whether an undertaking is conducted honestly and in the public interest unless it knows the facts. Notwithstanding incidental
disadvantages, the financial operations and other significant
facts about every business should be fully disclosed to the
public. There are certain matters, such as records of employees, inventions or processes under development, and properly confidential relations with suppliers and customers,
which in some cases should be private. Yet scarcely anything
would be so conducive to economic soundness and morality as
completely open fiscal and related records. Unfair profits
and privileges may be hidden by accounting secrecy. The
morbid fear of publicity from which business suffers is a chief
reason for public distrust of it. Many a well-conducted firm
or corporation has had public condemnation because the public did not know the facts.

6. *Business Competence.* To be thoroughly competent in
its own field is a primary duty of business. Everyone concerned with a business should continually study the business
as a whole and his part in it, and should acquire the best reasonably feasible ability in his work. Only when that is done
can business best serve the general good. The fact that a
business already is making money is no excuse for lack of
competence.

7. *Business Continuity.* The building of a business generally represents great effort and much ability on the part of
its originators, which should not be wasted. Also, employment in the undertaking becomes the chief capital of employees. They develop highly specialized abilities, acquire homes,
make friends and associates, and put down their roots around
the plant in which they work. The public comes to look to an
established business as a dependable source of supply, the

products or services of which can be bought with assurance of quality. The community in which a plant is located comes to count on it, to make investments because of it, and to develop interdependence. Its departure may wreck the community. All these facts create the duty of business continuity. If a company has actually finished serving its purpose, as a maker of horse-drawn cabs would have done, then, unless it can develop new products, it should close. But otherwise continuity and stability are desirable. The management should constantly seek to develop business understanding, judgment, and responsibility through the entire personnel. To insure continuity there should be constant searching for new blood, new managing ability, economy of operation, new products. The legal owners should realize that they did not build the business, but were leaders and guides to all those who built it together. The owners should not sell out a business to strangers just because they are tired or because they can make more money that way. They should strive to pass it on, very commonly without loss of its independence, to others who will similarly treat it as a trust for the employees, the community, and the public. To sell a business down river to those who have only an impersonal profit interest in it may be a betrayal of a public trust. Such betrayals for profit are frequently factors in great business consolidations.

8. Obligations to Employees. Business has obligations to employees beyond wage scales and working conditions. A normal, alert person, such as makes a good employee, has cravings, hopes and desires not greatly dissimilar to those of the owners. He wants dependable income and good working conditions, but also in many cases he wants his life to be an adventure, he craves to count in affairs, he would like to share in the making of policy and program. The business may be his life, just as it is the life of ownership and management, and much of the interest he gets out of life he must get through his relations with it. Good management will try to contribute fullness of life for its employees, insofar as this depends on normal industrial relationships. That does not mean that management should go outside its normal activities to provide activities or interests to employees.

Without being committed to any abstract and unrealistic theory about equality in industry, management should constantly explore its ranks for persons who have the character and interest to justify increased participation in the making of policies and programs and in sharing ownership. It is a commonplace observation that there is not enough initiative and enterprise in industry as a whole. Business should constantly search for these qualities latent in its personnel and encourage them to fullest development, so that employees shall not simply be faithful and obedient servants of management, but shall share in major responsibilities and opportunities. Even relatively small ability, where combined with genuine interest and responsibility, should be given participation to whatever extent is reasonably possible. Employees should be constantly searched for ability which is not being fully used. No employee should have reason to feel that he is in prison to his job. If the business does not offer reasonable exercise of an employee's ability he should be helped to find a better opportunity.

The attitude of collective bargaining, as between enemies, may be made unnecessary and obsolete by an attitude of associates working together for common ends. Because good business methods deserve fair conditions in which to succeed, a businessman who is trying to treat others as he would be treated should very carefully select his employees so that they will be persons who will respond to that attitude and will not take unfair advantage of it. An assumption that labor does not need organized representation should not be made unless conditions justify it, and in general that decision should be left to the employees directly concerned.

9. *Steady Operation.* Violent fluctuations of business are inherently wasteful. They deprive employees of security and predictable income. The community suffers from fluctuations of income. The quality of the product often is not maintained. Industry has the duty of trying to smooth out irregularities and of striving for reasonably uniform activity.

10. *Responsibility in Salesmanship, Advertising, and Representation of Goods or Services.* Representation of goods and services should be not only truthful, but representative,

and should be scrupulously fulfilled. Salesmanship should not go to the point of selling people what they do not need, or could get better elsewhere, or of overselling or of unbalancing the buyer's judgment. Salesmanship should be a process of mutual exploration of seller and buyer to discover the buyer's real need and interest.

11. Elimination of Waste. Waste of capital, labor, materials, or natural resources is in essence a waste of human life. Good management will try to eliminate waste in every form. It will not acquiesce in deliberate restriction of reasonable output. It will not wastefully change models or styles just to get more of the customer's money; it will not pander to low taste or morals under the guise of "giving the people what they want." Good business will not demean itself by encouraging waste on the part of its customers in order to increase its profits. It will not play upon foolish pride or ostentatious living.

12. Avoidance of Excesses. Good business will avoid excesses of every kind. It will not make excessive effort to grow big at the cost of quality or of putting undue strains on honest and competent competitors. It will not encourage excessive buying, excessive credit, overstimulation of sales which upset economic stability. It will not put its workers or its salesmen under excessive strain. It will undertake to keep its activities within the limits of wholesome, normal living.

13. Fair Competition. Good business will not avoid honest competition by seeking privileges or immunities or by secret agreements to manipulate prices or by effort to create monopolies. It will not try to destroy competition by excessive advertising. It will not practice competition by bad faith, deception, fraud, bribery, coercion of buyer or seller, or by embarrassing or taking advantage of competitors. It will rely for success on the quality of its goods and services and on their honest presentation to the public.

14. Cooperation. There are many ways in which a business, especially a small business, cannot act in the best manner by acting alone. In such cases economic cooperation and association are desirable or necessary. An entire industry or a group of firms can set up standards and enforce them, and can carry on research, beyond the ability of any member. It can provide technical training. It can open up new markets and perhaps find new sources of materials. It can supply market information. For helping to make small business units efficient, a reservoir of central services is imperative, because each small business of itself cannot afford a high order of such service. Central services can be provided by the co-operative action of many small firms, or they may be supplied by private central service organizations, such as are emerging in America. Central service associations may add to the efficiency of operation and may raise the standards of competition.

15. *Reconciliation of Controversies.* Good business will endeavor to resolve controversies, not by clever strategy or manipulation, but by open and sincere inquiry into the merits of issues, and by action in accordance with the merits. Arbitration should be favored before resorting to legal conflict or industrial strife.

16. *Restraint on Personal Ambition.* As in every other field, individuals and organizations need to guard against excess of personal ambition. The mainspring of business should be desire to have a useful and honorable part in the world's work, not desire for prestige, power and prominence. Every important business act needs to be examined for its motives.

17. *Control of Size.* Size of itself has certain effects. In some operations, such as railroads, mail and telephone, large size is important to full usefulness. In other cases, as in automotive manufacture or in steel production, large size seems to be necessary to efficiency. In much of business, however, size is not necessary for efficiency, and is not in the public interest. It tends to reduce the number of independent citizens, it tends to produce arbitrariness and dull uniformity, it tends to create irresponsible and unmanageable power, it sometimes coerces sources of supply, its power of publicity tends to give it the market somewhat irrespective of relative merit, it tends to monopoly with tendency to resultant higher prices, it tends to great concentration of wealth and to social stratification. What is very important, it tends to destroy community life and communities themselves.

Therefore, it is the duty of business not to grow larger than is economically and socially most productive, nor to sell out to trusts and combinations for the sake of manipulative profit. It should further public and legislative policy which will check abnormal, uneconomic, or socially unproductive growth.

18. Desirable Incentives. The chief reward of business is not exceptional income which puts its owners or managers into a favored social and economic class, but the opportunity to have an honorable part in the necessary and useful work of the world, and an honorable part in the total process of living. Only as private enterprise comes to realize and to live and work by this aim will it have the full respect of men and be safe against regimentation or confiscation by government.

The idea that business cannot thrive by this motive, and that businessmen could not greatly enjoy life under it, is an ancient myth that has done great harm and has greatly spoiled the lives of many businessmen and of their children. No enterpriser can say these motives are not sound until he has limited himself to a moderate income, has prepared himself as well as he can, has limited his undertakings to what a man of his abilities and resources can hope to handle effectively, and has done all he can to make honest business succeed.

A very large part of American business actually lives and works from the motive of wanting to take an honorable part in the world's work. It is chiefly that attitude which has given it its strength and such respect as it has had with the American people.

19. The Right Relation of Business to Other Interests. In the past many businessmen have had too low an opinion of their calling. For instance, factories were often dirty, ill-kept places, surrounded by junk, and with no effort at neatness or cleanliness. Then to show their interest in better things, industrialists would found art galleries or give public parks to their communities. More than half a century ago the National Cash Register Company of Dayton pioneered in making factories clean and attractive inside, with buildings and grounds as dignified and beautiful as a college campus. This course proved to be economical as well as socially desirable. The practice is becoming common as businessmen realize that industry is not an ugly thing to be used for making money with which to create beauty, but can itself satisfy the desire for a good environment.

Men are learning that business need not look up to the church as something finer and nobler, but that the practice of treating other people as one wants to be treated is a much more important and self-respecting process than living a sheltered life while talking about the golden rule from the pulpit.

In short, business should not be separated from the rest of life to live by its own rule of "business is business," with the one purpose of making money. It is an inseparable part of life, and should be in harmony with life as a whole. A good business platform is no more and no less than a good platform for living, with special application to business relationships.

As boys and girls in a small community see private enterprise around them they judge what life is like by what they see. What they hear in school or in church may be to them only talk or make-believe. What they see going on in economic life is to them the real thing. It is by watching business, they believe, that they can learn what life is really like. Thus business, next to the family, is often the most important educational force in the community, far more influential in actually determining people's habits than is either the school or the church. The standards by which it is conducted become the actual standards for society. Business is not only supplying goods and making money. It is in fact largely determining the pattern by which society will live and act. It therefore has a high degree of responsibility for the character of that pattern, and should be as interested in what that pattern *might be* as in what it is at present.

Economic Independence and Interdependence in the Community of the Future. In the earliest days each village was largely a little world by itself. It met its own needs or went without. In general in the western world today, small communities find themselves at the other extreme. Each produces for sale one or a few major products, and from the income received supplies its many needs from outside. There is little economic independence, and nearly complete interdependence.

Many people think of this new condition as permanent. However, it may possibly be a transition state, and perhaps we may look forward to a time when the individual small community may again have a considerable degree of economic autonomy.

Now the cost to the average householder of electric power generated, transmitted and distributed by the large central company commonly is not more than ten per cent under the cost of generation and distribution by a local community plant. Even now the relative cost of locally administered and centrally administered service depends more on efficiency of local administration than on the wholesale cost of power. Within a few decades atomic energy may make possible local autonomy in energy supply.

As the new world of technology and social development matures we may have increased community economic independence in several respects, and at the same time increased interdependence in others. A wise course will not lead back toward primitive, uneconomic methods, but will try to make the best economic and social use of possibilities.

A considerable degree of local self-sufficiency will be desirable for three reasons. First, it is by living together, working together and sharing life together that a collection of people becomes a living community. Physical proximity alone will not insure that. A thousand people living in a metropolitan apartment house may be almost complete strangers. Even members of the individual families, going their diverse ways in the morning and meeting briefly again in the evening, may be quite largely strangers to each other. People earning their livings in the same economic setting in the home town, or sharing in the same public operation, are more apt to be friends and neighbors.

Second: If local economic undertakings are locally owned, independent civic leadership may be present which would be largely absent or subservient if the community should live by employment in branch industries owned and controlled from a distance. If local industry is locally owned, business capacity and leadership will have something to do at home, and there will be less necessity for going to the distant city to find opportunity.

Third: The small community needs capacity for a considerable degree of independent economic activity, especially in case of depression. The greatest degree of confidence Americans ever had in the mastery of our economy was in the late nineteen-twenties, just before the greatest depression in our national history. The economy is more delicately balanced now than it was then, and confidence in the uninterrupted continuance of prosperity may not be justified. Further periods of depression are not improbable.

Until recently most small towns still had a considerable degree of economic independence. In depressions the local activities and production helped to carry them through. Most communities today have lost many self-sustaining functions, and a recurrence of a depression such as that of the early nineteen-thirties would leave them even more helpless than they were then.

In a normal community a considerable part of the time and energy of the members is used in serving each other, somewhat independently of the national economy, though such service is paid for with the money of the country. In time of depression, when money largely disappears from circulation, there is general paralysis of this kind of local services because of the lack of a medium of exchange. The local intelligence, skill, strength and willingness to work have not suddenly disappeared, but are still there. The electrician would like to repair the wiring and the painter is ready to paint the houses; the barber would like to cut people's hair, and their hair continues to grow and to need cutting; the physicians and nurses would like to care for the sick, and people have not stopped getting sick. The farmers, dairymen and fruit growers of the surrounding area would like to continue to sell their products and the people would like to continue to eat; while the farmer would like to have his equipment repaired, his house painted, and his children's tonsils removed. The proprietor of the local machine shop sits at his door wishing for customers. The village employees would like to continue to keep the streets clean and the sewer system in good order.

The continuation in good condition of these local services is not quite independent of the national economy, since they would call for some outside expenditures such as for medicines, paint and books. However, the community is not absolutely without money, and these small expenditures could be cared for. But its local economy is greatly slowed down.

The local community should be able to release these local energies, to free them from this magic spell which keeps strong men idle and willing men inactive. There should be some means for freeing this local time, energy and other resources so that they are not under so complete servitude to the national or world economy.

Suppose, for instance, that a local community should have a system of exchange-credit coupons which would circulate *within the locality* for releasing community energies and resources. Then the legal tender money would be needed chiefly for paying for imports into the home town, for national, state and county taxes, and for services supplied from without. It is an old economic axiom that "bad money drives out good." That should be just the function of these local exchange-credit coupons. They should drive out the legal tender from its loafing around home, doing the local chores, and put it to work paying for the outside goods and services needed by the community. We used this device in "The Yellow Springs Exchange" in the depression of 1931, and did in some degree release the local energies.

Such a policy would be good for the country as a whole. If each particular community in the nation should be active in releasing its own resources without severely calling on the depression-scarce legal-tender money, then that legal tender would be more nearly enough to carry the intercommunity load of exchange.

To prevent the local medium of exchange from being hoarded and taken out of circulation it probably would be well to provide for its progressive depreciation, so that each person would pass it on as rapidly as possible in order to share as little as possible in its depreciation. It would then serve the ideal function, as a medium of exchange, and not as a form of property to be hoarded. If people want to save, let them do so by using their exchange credit to buy and improve durable goods or land or houses, which at such times are a drug on the market. Houses built during the great depression are now worth several times what they cost. By such means a community, even in a severe depression, might have a highly active local economy in those activities which use chiefly local resources, and much of the local economic need could be met.

In thinking of the community of the future we may do well to keep in mind the desirability of maintaining a degree of self-sufficiency, not only in depression but in normal times, which would enable it to use some of its local resources of manpower and materials somewhat independently of the general prevailing economy. In time of prosperity this may seem an idle fantasy, yet as a principle of action it is important.

A community which has lost all economic independence of action is no longer fully a community, but is in part an economic vassal, and in the economic sphere will have a temper either of servitude or of rebellion against servitude. A good community, like an individual, has a degree of individuality and of self-direction. If an individual completely loses self-direction in any field he has lost some of his personality. The same is true of a community. With it, as with an individual, a degree of independence should exist along with a large element of interdependence. Complete self-sufficiency for individual or community is worse than an idle dream.

In thinking of where one will choose to live and make his living and bring up children, one consideration may well be whether the community of one's choice has a degree of economic independence with resulting increase of economic stability, as well as a degree of economic interdependence in the interest of more adequate variety of living and of more cosmopolitan outlook and interests.

How May a Small Community Be Industrialized?   The conventional and unimaginative habit of present-day America is to search for an existing industry which will favor the town by locating in it, often on condition of payment of a financial subsidy. This practice has continued for nearly a century, while all the time the young energy and intelligence in the home town which might be discovered, trained and helped to create industries, is ignored.

Rarely is there much inquiry as to whether the economic philosophy and the social attitude of the invited industry are in harmony with those of the local population. Often the community is not aware of having a philosophy or a spirit which deserves perpetuation or strengthening.

The community of the future will have character and personality which it will have achieved by a process of growth and discipline, much as an individual develops character and personality through purposeful living. It will want its industry to be, not something casually attached to it just for the sake of increased employment and income. It will want its industrial life to be a harmonious element in the fulfillment and enlargement of its personality. Insofar as is feasible it will prefer that its economic activity shall be a growth from within its own life, though it will always welcome from abroad what is in harmony with its essential quality.

Especially, the community of the future will know its own people, especially its boys and girls in their growth toward maturity. They will be helped in their search for suitable callings, and where necessary will have local financial assistance in preparing for them. Sometimes the best opportunities will be away from home, and in such cases there will be no effort to hold a person to his home town. In many cases, however, the work for which a young person is best fitted may be located as well in the home community as anywhere else. To the extent that the young people of a community have potential capacity for self-direction and leadership, and where an individual or a group of individuals would like to develop their own undertaking, the community may help them to do so, possibly helping them to secure preparatory training and experience elsewhere, and then providing the necessary finance for their undertaking. It is largely out of its own life that the industrialization of a community should take place, though often rigorous training and apprenticeship away from home may be necessary in preparation.

From among the endless variety of industrial and other economic possibilities in America some will be found that harmonize with the spirit and circumstances of the community. The mass character, and the geographical concentration, of economic effort in our country are less the results of inherent limitations of opportunity than of limitations of imagination, curiosity, spirit of adventure, and realization of possibilities.

And these are not wholly limited by inborn traits. Originality grows by imitation. Where a spirit of imagination, curiosity or adventure is present, it spreads to others who have it potentially, but in whom it had not previously been aroused. If a community as a matter of continuing policy is exploring the capacity of its own young people, and the varied possibilities of the industrial and economic scene, not only will possibilities be matched by opportunities, but the spirit will be one of interest, and expectation.

If a discriminating ethical and social spirit is in control, the local industries which grow up will come to have the community character. There will be little danger of "inbreeding." There are many live spirits in the country which are eager to find homes in a congenial atmosphere. As a village and its industries come to have distinct character and personality, they will attract others with similar standards, but with varied outlooks and backgrounds.

The question frequently arises as to whether a small community can compete with great metropolitan organizations in securing first-class minds in research and other phases of industry. In today's scientific and technical press we read frantic and almost fantastic appeals for scientists to work in industrial research laboratories. Incentives are spelled out in detail, such as "unlimited opportunity," "touching shoulders with great men," "rewards unlimited," "work on the frontiers of science," high and rapidly mounting salaries, "yachting on the sound," swimming, boating, mountain climbing, big-league baseball, moving expenses paid, profit-sharing, pensions, etc. Very seldom are fine community relations mentioned.

Recently a locally owned Yellow Springs firm placed an advertisement for a research scientist for a demanding job. It specifically stated that many of these spectacular incentives would be lacking, but that there was a difficult job, with hard work at moderate pay, located in a fine, human, small community. The outcome of this advertisement was applications from three or four persons who were so satisfactory that it was difficult to choose among them. The person employed, who was located from still another source, took the position at a substantial reduction from his former high salary, in considerable part because the family was impressed by the community as a place to live and rear a family. Another employer of well qualified research scientists in the same community stated recently that his firm never had lost one of its considerable research staff. The appeal of the village life was given as a major incentive for this absence of turnover.

Perhaps in more cases than are realized a major life interest of intelligent and purposeful men and women is in the conditions in which families live and children are reared. Perhaps the best and surest way to industrialize a small community which needs that part of its life expanded is to make it the kind of place where intelligent, purposeful people would like to live. If that course is taken, the young people native to the community may prefer to stay there, and others not so favorably placed will desire to come to it.

What Kinds of Small Industries Are Best for Small Communities? As a small community looks toward the future and undertakes to have a place in the general industry of the country, the kinds of industrial activities in which it engages may have much to do with its prospects for lasting success. In some industries small units may have good prospects. There are other industries with which a discriminating small community probably should have nothing to do.

Except in some cases for local consumption, industries which run to mass production and mass sales are poor prospects. In view of the mass production, the highly organized distribution, and especially the mass advertising, of General Motors storage batteries, it is doubtful whether a new small-scale automobile battery producer could succeed, almost regardless of the quality of his product. Somewhat the same would be true for soap and washing powders, and house paints. Mass advertising by large corporations may drown out small firms with equal or better product. In fact, this may be as near to economic violence as small firms are apt to meet.

Some products may call for such inherently large-scale operation as to preclude small-scale success. Automobiles and railway locomotives are examples. Some products would have so few market openings as to be precarious reliances. Automobile parts might have only half a dozen possible purchasers. Even though at first such a business might be profitable, its continuing success would be very uncertain—its product might suddenly be displaced by an alternative, or by the great manufacturer undertaking to produce its own parts.

There are other products which are largely immune to such specific dangers. The little industries of Yellow Springs illustrate types which may have fair prospect of surviving under present-day industrial conditions. There is the stained-glass studio, designing and producing windows for churches and other buildings. These are sold, not chiefly by advertising, but from the reputation of the firm among architects, by word of mouth and through prospective customers' visiting. The Antioch Bookplate Company produces perhaps 90% of the bookplates in the country. More than thirty firms, large and small, have undertaken to compete, and then have ceased. Total sales are not great enough to justify maintenance of a department by a large firm, while the possession of modern equipment, development of trade channels, and reputation for quality make it hard for a small, new operator to compete.

The Yellow Springs Instrument Company makes electronic devices for laboratories, for the Atomic Energy Commission, industrial laboratories, medical clinics, and a wide variety of users. It depends on word-of-mouth reputation, personal visits by salesmen, distribution through scientific instrument distributers, etc., more than on mass advertising. The Bolle woodworking plant does custom cabinet and mill work for educational and industrial plants, where high quality of work and the proximity of the customer are important. The Vie Design Studios do industrial designing, in which word-of-mouth publicity and personal contact are more effective than advertising, and where the possible market is very widely scattered.

The Velsey Company, making "stone surface plates," supplies laboratories—governmental, industrial and educational. Their sales are made largely through a distribution agency. The Mazzolini Art Bronze Foundry receives individual orders from artists, architects, building commissions and others, on the basis of direct reputation. The Vernay Laboratories sell to manufacturers of washing machines, automobiles, and many industries. With a business of $2,000,000 a year, until recently they have not had a sales force, nor advertised. The Morris Bean foundry sells aluminum castings to a varied lot of industries, large and small. They furnish perhaps two thirds or three quarters of all the automobile tire molds made in America, simply by out-competing larger companies in quality and price. Dewine and Hamma, with a business of about $3,000,000 a year, sell farm seeds to a large number of wholesalers. Since in farming, seed is a small part of the total cost, quality is all-important, and a gradually acquired reputation for quality is the basis of continued business. The Antioch Press does most of the printing for Antioch College, and prints a considerable number of magazines of limited circulation. "Kip Productions" makes educational films.

Not one of these industries depends on widespread advertising to the general public; not one depends on selling its product to one or a few large consumers (except as the Antioch Press sells printing to Antioch College); not one produces an item of current vogue or fancy, for which the demand may suddenly disappear; scarcely any are competing with big, nationwide corporations. During the same period we have seen distress and failure come to well-managed small industries which undertook to compete with industries having nationwide distribution systems and using mass advertising. Not one of our little industries depends on high tariff walls.

In the vast perimeter of American industry and specialized services, the variety of possibility for small businesses, many of them suitable for small communities, is almost without limit. Even very mediocre competence may have good prospect for success provided the demands of the undertaking are not out of proportion to the degree of competence available.

Twenty-five years ago it used commonly to be said that nineteen out of twenty commercial and industrial undertakings were failures. In the small community industries of Yellow Springs during the past quarter-century there have been three times as many successes as failures. In nearly every case the failure has come in the initial stages, and most of them were little more than incidents on the way to success. The many possible causes of failure should inspire caution and forethought, but not timidity or paralysis of effort. Many a successful effort has broken the rules of caution, but it is important to distinguish rashness from courage. C. F. Kettering remarked that a chief reason for the industrial progress of America has been that Americans are not afraid to risk failure.

It might be misleading to conclude a discussion of small community industries without emphasizing the difficulties attending their establishment today. Up to recent years a young industry might grow out of its earnings. Today the heavy income tax makes that more difficult. Minimum wage laws largely prevent a small industry from locating in a place of low living costs and paying correspondingly low wages while getting on its feet. The relatively low federal capital gains tax makes it more profitable in many cases for the owners of a profitable small industry to sell to a large industry, and to live on the profits of the sale, than to continue to operate even at a good profit. A sound firm which is temporarily "in the red" may be purchased by a large, very profitable company because the losses of the small firm can then be used to reduce the income tax of the large organization.

In some fields mass national advertising by very large firms may smother and extinguish a small competitor, almost regardless of the relative merits of the products. In time of scarcity of materials the great corporations have the influence to obtain the limited supplies, leaving small firms to fail for lack of materials. When a great corporation finds need for a patented process used by a small company it can make any offer it pleases, and if that is not accepted it may infringe the patent and use the process. What chance has the little industry against the big legal staff much experienced in legal manipulation? Big industry, in its effort to diversify is going into fields formerly thought of as small. The recruiting staff of a large corporation can search colleges for promising graduates before the small industry gets a chance at them.

These are serious obstacles, and this is by no means a complete list. Rather than comment on them one by one we may say that thirty years ago similar formidable difficulties were presented to a person considering the starting of a small industry. He was told that the day of small business was past. Yet a very considerable part of the successful small industries of today have originated since that time.

XII

Education in the Community of the Future

When the Progressive Education Association was formed in 1921 I was appointed its first president, though I was not present. At that time I was traveling actively, and used that opportunity to try to become acquainted with the field. I found that the persons who originated the organization and were guiding its destiny were unconscious disciples of Rousseau. To them a child was an organism of divine and unmarred potentialities which, if given full freedom, would grow into a perfect, rightly proportioned personality. What it chiefly needed, they believed, was freedom, and shelter from the suppressions and distortions of social conditioning. As that position became clear I withdrew my interest from the organization.

While I was actively exploring the possibilities of this new association I read an article by the head of a famous American private school. He stated that he had little concern about the interests of a boy who was sent to him. He knew what constituted good education and good character, and any boy under his direction would be put through a process of discipline and training which would transform him into what the cultured American of good character should be. To this man a boy was a lump of formless clay, except when some of his "nature" appeared as hard lumps or bits of gravel which resisted molding. Under his discipline all this would be ground to uniform consistency, and then molded and furnace fired to a fine, tough, enduring shape, that of the proper American. This process is very effective. As used at West Point in earlier decades it received miscellaneous intelligent, vigorous Americans, and by relentless, formal discipline, with long-time inbreeding of the teaching staff, turned all but a few of the more resisting ones into a type patterned after the antidemocratic Prussian army of a century and a half ago. To do this in a free country like America was a real achievement, and testified to the practical efficacy of the process.

I find myself not in sympathy with either one of these philosophies of education. In the chapter on the evolution of social controls I have presented the view that human personality is a complex result of the interaction of inborn animal traits, of cultural tradition, and of critical inquiry with creative thinking. No one of these elements should have the free right of way, and no one of them should be neglected or eliminated. The child is not the cluster of ideal, inborn potentialities that was envisioned by the originators of the Progressive Education Association (the philosophy of the organization later went through a considerable metamorphosis). It is more like a raw material being given both form and substance as it comes into contact with the prevailing cultural inheritance. As some parts of the cultural tradition are more desirable than others, constant appraisal and selection are necessary. Much of the inborn nature remains, which is partly essential to survival, partly desirable but not absolutely essential, partly undesirable but not seriously harmful, and partly outdated and a menace to survival. The inborn drives should be partly encouraged, partly tolerated, partly discouraged, and to some extent rigorously eliminated. Both inborn traits and the cultural inheritance require to be appraised and disciplined by critical reason and inquiry, which itself is fallible and liable to error. Yet there are inborn drives and cultural traditions of freedom which should be respected.

To the extent that this appraisal is sound it is inevitable that opinions concerning education should vary greatly. They will be influenced by variations of cultural background and experiences. Such wholesome unity as does emerge will be largely the result of free inquiry and the critical appraisal of experience and of inborn traits. Simple uniformity in outlook does not necessarily imply the truth of that on which people agree. When nearly the whole world believed in witches there probably were no more witches around than there are today in America where few people believe in them.

The American system of elementary education was borrowed, largely from Germany, when it had not been long in existence there. While in this country it has effloresced into greater "richness" and complexity, the fundamental design has not changed. For millions of years the way in which the young of the human species and their immediate forebears were educated was by living in the community and absorbing the common culture by intimate contact with it and participation in it. Our present-day elementary and secondary education consists of taking boys and girls out of the living culture of their communities and pumping into them certain elements abstracted from that culture, not by participating in it, but by the second-hand process of learning from books what some persons have written about it.

We never should expect a boy to grow up to be an exceptionally good baseball player if he should study about it in books for eight years of elementary and four years of high school without ever playing a game; yet we expect young people to learn life in that way. We doubtless need to improve on the age-old ways of learning, and to use specialists as teachers. Yet we should not be driven to a choice between this way and that. They should be combined so that boys and girls in the process of education should actually be participating in the process of everyday living, but should supplement or interweave such experience with elements that are best transmitted more formally. The present-day trend toward consolidated schools makes participation in the common life more difficult and more restricted than ever.

It is my hope that in the community of the future childhood and youth will have far greater freedom so far as regimentation of hours and days and weeks is concerned. Growing boys and girls should have much greater freedom to be out of doors, and to be working at home and at what the people of the community work at. Then they should be under a far stronger discipline than now in the cultural tradition of community living —in considerateness, courtesy, integrity, courage, stamina, responsibility and good will. This discipline will come, not often by learning rules and being punished for infractions, but by participating intimately and for a considerable part of the time in the life of a community where those traits prevail.

An experience I once had in living with a Black Forest family from South Germany illustrates the educational value of the common life. The parents, six children and the grandmother constituted what might be called an organic family. Though their family life moved through the days and weeks with a

smooth effectiveness which might have come from disciplined
rehearsal, there was no suggestion of teaching or direction.
It seemed to flow naturally. After the evening meal the entire
family would be at work. Grandmother would knit, the younger
daughter would spin. The youngest children had their part,
especially around meal time. The four- or five-year-olds
were actually useful. Work was not unpleasant or a burden.
It seemed as natural as breathing. It was the survival of an
ancient culture.

A Hopi Indian household is similarly a self-directing group.
No one exercises authority, or tells others what to do, or when
or how. All members fall naturally into a pattern in which the
abilities of each serve the needs of all.

There have been many families and communities where
such conditions existed, and many of our best men and women
have come from them. However, both our economic life and
our educational life tend to break such a pattern. When the
pattern has been thoroughly broken, trying to renew it is a little
like putting Humpty Dumpty together again. Wherever real
community still exists we have the possibility and opportunity
of preserving it and encouraging its growth and multiplication,
so that the precious tradition shall not be lost.

In his later years Mahatma Gandhi developed a process of
elementary and secondary education which consisted largely
of having boys and girls share in the normal life of the community under the guidance of able and devoted men and women.
What we call formal education was not omitted, but was blended
and integrated with this participation in living. Descriptions
of this process and a syllabus for the first eight years can be
supplied by Community Service, Inc.

So-called "progressive education" undertook some elements of such a program, but in many cases these methods
were so mixed with soft living and indulgence that sometimes
the results were not all that might be desired. As an example
of primitive, age-old education, American Indian boys of the
West were not soft. They competed in endurance, toughness
and resistance to pain. They were very highly self-disciplined.
We should be able to devise better forms of discipline, but a
less formal and more natural course for education of boys and
girls need have no relation to softness.

Child labor has been largely abolished because it was so commonly associated with economic exploitation; but there is no better way to learn what life is like than for boys and girls to work along with their elders wherever the work makes that feasible. Such labor should not have the regimentation of long hours that is usually associated with industry, or even with attendance at school. There again we have broken the pattern, and may have great difficulty in renewing it. Karl Marx, who would have been far from approving economic exploitation of children, was emphatic and explicit in holding that, with danger of economic exploitation removed, child labor should be an integral and important element of education. Taking part in the productive life of the community should not monopolize the time of childhood. A boy or girl needs ample time to "loaf and invite the soul." Sheer freedom for time to grow should be provided as it is not by present school programs.

The literature of education is nearly endless, and any effort to give an orderly treatment of the subject in a discussion of the community of the future would be futile. What we wish to indicate is that in the good community of the future there will be an effort to recover the unity of life. Education, economics, religion, recreation and other interests will be parts of a single pattern; a pattern which does not introduce dogmatism or arbitrary regimentation, but provides opportunity for the living together of free men. Education, and especially elementary and secondary education, as now practiced, tends to separate childhood and youth from the general processes of living. They become in some degree a separate culture, cut off from the common life, and often in rebellion against it. The great mass of criticism of education commonly points out some of the symptoms of failure of education, but only rarely refers to the basic condition of formal education, that the life of childhood and youth is largely cut off from the common life.

The community of the future will need to take a new look at the fundamental processes of education. Our present methods in their fundamentals were established before the concept of life as a process of evolution had arisen, before the biologist even knew of the existence of the cell, before modern psychology, sociology and anthropology were born. We need to view it anew in the light of present knowledge and insight.

XIII

Religion in the Community of the Future

What have Religion and Community to do with each other? The affairs of the day and of the year take most of our attention and interest; yet men crave general purpose and direction. They seek associations and influences which will help them to hold to their better purposes and to define their aims. The total of those elements which contribute to that end we may call religion.

Since the family and the community are the associations in which children get the major directions for their lives, they should be the center and home of religious life. Many influences from without—literature, tradition, customs and creeds—are valuable for guidance, for enlightenment and for inspiration, but should not be authority. As Bryant said of human reason, "She should be my counselor, but not my tyrant." In a free society the determination of purpose and direction should be from the individual outward, not imposed from without, though the wise individual will use all the resources of understanding and motive that are available.

The life of the individual will be richer and fuller if he has worked out his own way of life than if he has uncritically accepted a pattern handed to him. Similarly the community will have a fuller life if it assumes the responsibility for its own character and purposefulness, rather than if it subscribes to some external authority.

The unity and community loyalty which will exist in the good community of the future will not result from the suppression of individual purpose; but from realization by free, intelligent, purposeful individuals that men are interdependent, social beings, and that if their purposes are right they will be in harmony with the right purposes of the community. Similarly, the unity of the community with larger societies, such as the nation, will result, not from the subordination of community purposes to those of the nation, but to realization that the right purposes of the one will be in accord with the right purposes of the other. Sincere, intelligent, inclusive purposefulness on any level is identical with ethical action. The respect and consideration which the individual, the family and the community will give to the standards of larger free social units will rest on the realization of the greater duration and wider range of experience of the larger units. That respect and consideration will not extend to authoritarianism and tyranny of body or mind, however old or widespread. Suppression of freedom of mind or body is not validated by its long duration.

In religion, as elsewhere, the life of the community will suffer if the direction of its spiritual life is taken away, and rests at a distance. We repeat, in religion, as in economics, education, and government, wherever the community gives up self-direction in matters where it has reasonable capacity for self-direction, occasion for common community experience is reduced, and the personality and character of the community are less. In America it is not accidental that some of those religious fellowships that have had local or "congregational" government have been the sources of the movements in religion which have most fully profited from the increase of human insight and understanding during recent centuries.

As a picture of what religion may be in the community of the future, let us point to what it was in certain communities of the past. Parts of mountainous Switzerland never were completely submerged by empire and outward authority, in either religion or government, though only in special circumstances did the spirit of freedom become sufficiently influential or audible to be clearly recorded in history.

Many years ago my wife and I spent some time in the high Swiss valleys above Berne. Here religion was free. No outside authority dictated creed or form. The local pastor, a humble, hard-working, spiritual man, lived and worked in that freedom. Since he had no auto, we provided transportation about his parish, and so got intimate glimpses of home and small group life. Living conditions in the mountain valleys were very hard, but were made less difficult by the pervading quality of friendship and community. The pastor and the peo-

ple were deeply religious, but not narrowly so. The spirit of
free study and inquiry kept open the windows of their minds.
In their religious meetings they studied the lives of great
spiritual leaders, of both Christian and other faiths. Their
interests ranged over many fields, with their pastor as leader
in the application of their view of life to agriculture, arts,
crafts, music, literature and sheer recreation. The cultural
tradition preserved friendship, considerateness and social
responsibility. Uniformity of belief was not made a requirement of community recognition. When I think of what religion
in the community might be like, my mind goes back to that
Swiss mountain valley.

The religious life of a community may be a source of either
unity and community spirit, or faction and separateness. In
many towns and villages in our country the various religious
fellowships, while active and loyal in their own spheres, see
themselves and their members as parts of the whole community. Where any activity pertains to the whole they seek to
share in it, rather than to dominate it or to split it into its
denominational segments. This is especially the case when
policy is not dictated by outside authority.

In other cases there is effort on the part of each religious
fellowship to make itself a closed community, with as many
activities as possible centered in the separate congregations,
rather than in the community as a whole. In some cases there
is effort of a religious organization to isolate the minds of
its adherents from other outlooks than its own. Too often in
American small towns the competing church organizations
have been destroyers of unity.

The community should not be a monolithic structure with
no relationships except between the individual and the community. It is at its best a network of smaller and still more
intimate associations. But each of these should see itself,
not as living its own life in separateness, but as contributing
to the life as a whole, with many interrelationships among its
elements. The unity which arises from such relationships is
that of free choice, not of compulsion or regimentation. Religious fellowships should be a part of this free play of good
will and social responsibility.

Religion is not an obsolescent element of living. In the desire to live well and purposefully men need association to keep alive the fire of aspiration, and for counsel, cooperation and fellowship. In religion, as elsewhere, man is a social creature. Even where one has achieved new insight in solitude he can transmit it to others best in society. Religious association should be a carrier of a very precious part of the social tradition.

In a good society there is no sharp division between the sacred and the secular. If government is administered in a spirit of good will, integrity and justice; if business is conducted, not chiefly for self-interest, but as a way for contributing to the general economic welfare; if personal conduct is motivated by a desire to further the soundness, the dignity, the sensitivity and the purposefulness of life; if self-expression in art and literature have similar motivation; then the need for religion as a remedial force grows less.

There remains the normal function of pioneering in ethical and spiritual values and in strengthening the purposes and increasing the aspirations of its participants. Finer patterns of life and thought must first win their way and be exemplified in the lives of strongly purposeful members of small groups before they can be passed on by example. It is when people see a better way of life in practice that they come to care for it. To this end a religious fellowship may be creative and productive, acting somewhat as a research and pilot community within the larger community—not as separate from it, but as pathfinder for it.

When we come to the supernatural and theological aspects of religion, they differ so greatly and so fundamentally in the different religions that a discussion of them seems outside the range of the present inquiry.

XIV

Recreation in the Community of the Future

Recreation is a necessary and important element in living, and adequate provision should be made for it. There are several values in play. First, it can be an end in itself, an experience in the sheer joy of living.

Second, it can be training or activity in the arts of life. Nature is shrewd and plays tricks. She slips her practical purpose into actions which seem to be ends in themselves. A little girl plays with her doll simply because she likes playing with dolls; yet in the very process she is learning how to take care of babies. A large part of the toys of childhood are but small models of what men use for utilitarian purposes.

Nature tries to put joy in life, by making us like to do the things we ought to do. To use the biologist's language, those forms tend to emerge which are well adjusted or harmonious in themselves, because such forms have better probability for survival. If a creature wants to do and gets joy in doing what it needs to do to survive, it is more apt to do that thing. Why do normal vigorous boys like to hunt and fish ? Because through several millions of years their ancestors made their livings that way, and became well adjusted to it. Why do fewer boys and men take similar joy in farming and gardening? Because men have practiced agriculture for only perhaps 15, 000 to 30, 000 years (these particular numbers are mostly a guess on my part), and in the slow process of evolution agriculture has not had time to become so deeply imbedded in our biological nature. The making of bows, arrowheads, and stone axes is much older than agriculture, and so more boys and men would rather play at tinkering with tools than play at farming. There probably are more "do-it-yourself" men with tools than there are men who get their recreation in gardening. But some love both. Many a lawyer and businessman subconsciously tries to "get back to nature" by buying a farm; and since men have had cattle for a much longer period than they have raised crops, many more gentleman farmers take pleasure in cattle raising than in raising wheat or corn. Thus do we hark back to nature.

Third, play is a chief means of bodily and mental exercise. In normal life it is largely through play that boys and girls achieve bodily development, and it may contribute much to mental growth. So here again nature slips her purpose into play. It is largely by social play that boys and girls become social beings. They learn how human beings behave, they develop the arts of association, they learn resilience under human stresses. They relate themselves to society.

Then, as men and women grow older, recreation is just what the word implies—re-creation. Most labor, either of body or of mind, has much in it that is repetitive. We become muscle-bound and spirit-bound, not so much men and women as implements of production. With suitable recreation, we cease for a time being bricklayers or lawyers or milliners or housewives or grocers, and become men and women. It is largely by recreation that we remain human.

Perhaps the most frequent use of what commonly is called recreation is to help shorten life. If our lives are without purpose or design, then some way to get a little titillation of the senses, some way to make the hours pass more quickly, ranks high among our wants. Mass sports, at which we can be spectators, and routine, uncreative activities such as the twice-a-week bridge club, or—if we are very well-to-do— Monte Carlo and the lesser members of that species, may seem very necessary.

The community of the future will give as serious attention to recreation as to education—for it is a major element of education; as serious attention as to health—because it is a major means to health. It will not let religion crowd out recreation, for in no small degree it is by playing together that we enter into mutual understanding and companionship. It will balance economic life with recreation, for recreation is needed to free us from the tendency to permanent warps and atrophies of parts of our bodies and spirits which are imposed by the compulsions and repetitions of the daily work. In short, provisions for recreation will be an integral part of the pattern of the good community of the future.

Especially play is necessary for childhood. There is an old highbrow saying among biologists that "ontogeny recapitulates philogeny." What they mean is that as an individual develops from germ cell to maturity it takes the same course as that followed by its ancestors in the progress of evolution. The human embryo or fetus in its early stages has gills like a fish; later its body is covered with hair or fur. At birth its hands are very strong, though not quite strong enough to hold onto its mother as an ape does.

But that repetition of the past does not stop at birth. During his early years a boy is very much a wild animal. He is at home in the woods—hunting, fishing, camping, climbing trees. He needs space. One of the greatest inhumanities being practiced is the shutting up of vigorous growing boys for long hours each day in regimented schools, just when they most crave the out-of-doors. While this practice is less than a century old for most human families, we already take it as the course of nature, as for centuries the Chinese took the binding of girls' feet. Just as a cat brought up in an upper storey of a big city apartment may be afraid to step on the grass and may have no interest in mice, so a boy or girl similarly reared may have no taste for the out-of-doors, and may prefer the bookshelf, the television or the baseball grandstand.

The good community of the future will make adequate outdoor provision for the normal development of normal children, with a minimum of necessary restriction on freedom of physical movement, and with the variety of nature for a setting. There also will be provision for craft work and shop work which may be as valid to them as the making of bows and arrows and arrowheads was to the boyhood of their long-ago ancestors. And of course there will be provision for the various sports which rank high among the means for developing bodily and mental stamina, and training in social adjustment.

Even a century ago more than three quarters of our ancestors were rural dwellers as children, and had the whole out-of-doors for their playgrounds. In our plans for living we have not yet taken into account the great change of environment which has taken place.

Much of the playground equipment now furnished to children is plainly a makeshift substitute for the lack of normal play opportunity. A "jungle-gym" in the kindergarten yard is better than nothing, but very artificial, something like expecting a man to make love to the mannikin in the shop window. The good community will take seriously play and other recreation, making such provision for it that boys and girls will have opportunity for full development of body and social spirit.

Mature people also need recreation, and their lives would be fuller, more normal and happier if their play had more content. One of my most successful efforts to make provision for recreation was to provide a large craft shop in a construction camp, together with a well qualified furniture designer. Here many families would gather for entire evenings, making everything from pewter dishes to motor boats. The free play of conversation, counsel and mutual aid helped to turn a working force into a community. A good community will not omit conventional recreational resources, as for tennis, baseball, and volleyball, but it will find a far greater range of interests.

Our daily lives tend to confine us to fairly narrow channels of experience. Most of us crave a larger range. In a good society play will not be regimented. In our leisure we will find opportunity for activities that fill out our lives. No community can fulfill all the possibilities of leisure, but if there is freedom from conventional regimentation to a few kinds of activities, such as to conventional sports or conventional dancing, the range which will emerge will be large.

As I look around our little village I observe such variety. When a village art show was organized there were more than a hundred exhibitors, in a great variety of media—textiles, ceramics, photography, stained glass, printing, sculpture, cabinet work, painting, drawing, gardening, and others. On a pleasant spring or autumn day our village "green belt" of woods may have a hundred local visitors. Dramatics with a home theater has a large following. A considerable number of the villagers are gardeners. The village swimming pool is greatly in demand. The summer day camp for little children is popular. Family outings in the nearby woods are common. Baseball, basketball, volleyball, tennis and golf, all are present. Two men are among the nation's authorities on cave exploration. A few have a hobby of collecting mushrooms. Someone usually runs a nature column in the weekly paper. Of course there are the fishermen and the hunters. Another hobby is beekeeping. Short camping and canoe trips are popular. A school camp draws visitors from a considerable area. Music has varied expressions, including band and orchestra. Boy and girl scouts are active. Nature hikes are frequent. Folk dancing is common. A good many people travel, sometimes on very limited budgets, to Canada, Mexico, South America and Europe. Then there are the community undertakings: the annual "apple butter festival," Hallowe'en street carnival, etc.

It is not entirely an accident that there is not a stadium of any kind in the village, no equipment for spectators for baseball, basketball, football or any other sport, except for limited space in the high school gymnasium. Play is chiefly for the interest of the players.

Quite naturally, many people find little time for recreation because they have so many other interests. The joy of doing one's work when it is interesting is as strong today as it was with the hunter of the old stone age.

Reading is a major recreation. Good poetry or fine prose brings a joy akin to that of music. Good fiction keeps alive our emotions, and saves us from becoming automata or thinking machines. Good humor may save us from stomach ulcers. Books on travel may give us much the thrill of going ourselves.

Reading is a major recreation. Yet it may be that the library profession is mistaken in holding that reading of itself is good, and that trivial reading is better than none. Reading can be a way of escape from living, not much better than other escapes such as perpetual card playing or gossip or gambling or getting one's chief satisfaction in life from attending ball games. London is full of bookstores, and one gets the impression that for a considerable number of the customers, reading is almost the only way in which starved, anemic personalities get a sense of living. So far as quantity alone is concerned it does not trouble me that Americans are not great readers. It is just possible that they spend more time at living.

I shall not discuss particular forms of recreation, or try to outline organizations for initiating or administering recreation. The chapter on the physical setting of the community has suggestions on the acquisition of outdoor areas.

XV

Intentional Communities

There are three major approaches toward bringing about better communities and a better world. One of these is the process of violent revolution—the tearing to pieces of society as it is and the effort to rebuild it by a better pattern. The French Revolution has been the classic example. The second method is that of living within the communities we have, doing what we can to keep their better elements alive and strong, and gradually removing or improving what falls short of a good pattern. That is the way which seems open to most of us.

The third approach is by creating new communities or other societies by new and better patterns. This last method, the results of which in recent years have been given the name "intentional communities," is the subject of this chapter. It has been popular to smile at "utopian" or planned communities as freakish and futile efforts of erratic cults. Their place in history refutes that opinion. The great Greek world, extending from the Black Sea to Gibraltar, in no small degree was populated by deliberately designed colonies, some of them provided with "ideal" constitutions by recognized philosophers, and laid out by town planners. The old East Indian civilization was scattered over a wide area by deliberately planted colonies, as described by Nehru in his history of India. The Teutonic League planted its towns and cities by the score over eastern Europe beyond German borders, and the population of these deliberately planted colonies maintained their characteristic Germanic culture for many centuries, with a population which may have reached into millions. Intentional communities have been created through thousands of years, and have had great historic influence.

The method of patiently maintaining the good qualities and adding needed qualities to existing communities, and that of creating new ones, each has influence on the other. The United

States is the outcome of an intricate combination of both ways. Without the clear vision and the bold departures from the past which were made by the Puritan, Massachusetts Bay, Quaker, Anabaptist and other settlers who came with pioneer visions of a new society, the framers of our constitution could not have done their work, and the United States could not have made the great departure in history which it presented to the world.

Yet that new pattern had been long in preparation. The Lollard preachers whom Wyclif sent through rural England gave courage and direction to the ancient community patterns which the Norman conquest and its aftermath had so nearly destroyed in England; and indirectly through Huss, they did the same in eastern Europe. For two long centuries "The Seekers" in England, who were the outcome of Wyclif and the Lollards, in their rural communities struggled against the bitter persecution of the church to maintain their spiritual inheritance and to give clarity and form to a vision of a good way of life. They largely laid the foundation for the nongovernmental religious fellowships of England. It was largely the inheritors of that vision in England, and of the somewhat similar Anabaptist and related movements in Europe, who as settlers in America made the pattern in the new world different from that in the old. In Spanish America, where the settlers brought no such vision, how different has been the history!

The United States was settled, not only by these pioneers who had fairly clear visions of a new world, but by a far greater number who came with no other expectation than better living and perhaps greater freedom. So our country is closely bound to the many cultures, traditions and peoples from which it took its departures. We repeat, it is a fairly well established principle of genetics that the best prospect for biological advance is enough isolation and separateness to allow the fixing of a new type, combined with enough interbreeding with other types to provide a reservoir of genetic possibilities. We have suggested that a similar principle prevails in social relations. How closely our country has come to an optimum of such possibilities is a matter of opinion.

The creation of new communities, and the more deep-seated of the efforts for creation of new patterns and ways of life in and among existing communities, have been among the more important and universal ways in which societies the world over have maintained their vitality and have advanced in type. The casual drifting in of settlers into an undeveloped area, and their unthinking repetition of the pattern in which they grew up, may be as uncreative extension of the old as is the new swarm of bees starting in a new hive where it will reproduce a pattern of living which paleontologists tell us may not have been altered for 50,000,000 years.

The endeavors of groups of people to conceive and to establish new and better ways of life have been among the great creative forces in history. It has been customary to smile at these efforts because of the large percentage of failures. As we have already stated, of nature's efforts to establish new and continuing species at least nine out of ten are failures. We think of American business as being on the whole successful. Yet it used to be stated that of all American business ventures, only one in 20 avoided failure, which usually came during the early stages. The proportion of failures in the intentional communities of America probably has been somewhat less, and the rewards and fruits of those that have succeeded have extended to the furthest reaches of mankind. We might almost state it as an axiom that a considerable proportion of failure is natural to efforts for progress.

The greater and the more ambitious the departure from ways of the past that is contemplated by a community, the greater the burden of pioneering which it must assume. The community at first glance seems to be so elementary that there is little to it; just a grouping of houses, some means of economic support, provision for schools, churches, sanitation and water supply, and there you have it. The old-time town planner, if he could find a "focus" in the landscape for his physical design, would have little further trouble. One of our well-known town planners, asked to provide a plan for a city of 100,000 in the Far East, stopped by and did it over the weekend. A great handicap to all endeavors at building new patterns of community life and new communities is ignorance and even arrogance with regard to the nature of human society.

Pioneering in creating new ways of community life as a manner of progress by social change sometimes has been discredited because of poor and ill-defined motives, ignorance, narrowness, dogmatism and superficiality of endeavor. Just as these qualities characterize much of our prevailing society, so they extend into attempts at pioneering. Just as government agencies, industrialists and promoters commonly are heavy-handed in their efforts to build new communities in housing projects, industrial towns and resettlements, so are most of the venturesome radicals who have joined pioneering community undertakings. Often they mistake revolt for creativity. Just as Rousseau turned the church dogma of the innate depravity of man into the doctrine of the innate perfection of man, so some of these radical "pioneers" invert the conservative economic dogma of the sacredness of private property into the opposite dogma that private ownership of property is inherently evil; and the attitude of extreme individualism into the doctrine that the individual exists only for the community, state or church. Only rarely in America have intentional communities been moved by the aim of regaining for the community a whole, unwarped view of life.

But it is not primarily the lack of balance or completeness of design which is most fatal to intentional communities, but the dogmatic and blinding assumption which many deviants from prevailing society have that they know the one true way, and are traveling in it. Each group, each community, having some desirable part of a pattern which others lack, tends to be closed and isolated from the other values it needs. So great is our insecurity and our fear of losing hold of the little corner of truth we have grasped, and so great is the social pressure upon us from the world about us toward conformity and mediocrity, that we have lacked the poise and confidence to build a society of societies in which the strength and accomplishments of each supplement and complement those of others that are different.

It is not through putting all together in the melting pot that this isolation can best be overcome, but through association and interrelations among different culture groups and communities. Such interrelations between communities and cultures will lay the basis for social order within nations, and for international relations. That mutual understanding cannot be achieved chiefly through top-level actions by governments. It will be surest and most lasting when it grows out of the actions of individuals and communities that have come to recognize, respect and value each other's qualities.

Present-Day Intentional Communities. Recently there has been renewed interest in intentional communities. Some of them, such as the Jewish kibbutzim in Israel and the Christian orthodox "Bruderhof" in Paraguay, England and the United States, are extremely communal. Others, such as the French "Communities of Work," are economically communal, with some cultural community; still others show a wide range of community relationships, in some cases reduced to cooperative ownership of individual homes.

In the United States a number of small groups have united in a "Fellowship of Intentional Communities." The 30 or less members of this very loose organization vary widely in philosophy, character of organization, and in their prospects for survival. They have in common a desire to maintain a social and/or economic group which will be free from the regimentation of our conventional life. They want a new chance to create a new pattern. Beyond that there are few factors common to all the members.

The Hutterites, with about three thousand members in our northwestern states and western Canada, and the Society of Brothers (Bruderhof organization), are strongly orthodox Christian and very communal. The Amish fellowships, numbering about 25,000, tend to withdraw from the world. Both they and the Hutterites have about the highest birth rates in the world, and have gradually spread from small beginnings. Since they spread by buying adjoining farms they are sometimes disliked by their neighbors. South Dakota, where the Hutterites have been spreading by setting up new communities, has enacted legislation prohibiting them from buying more land. Such legislation is of doubtful validity. (Of these religious intentional communities, only the Bruderhof has had any affiliation with the Fellowship of Intentional Communities.)

By far the largest of what might be called intentional community organizations, the Mormons, with nearly a million members, have had strong social organization, but are becoming more and more like the prevailing American pattern, especially as they establish congregations in cities. The others have relatively small numbers.

It may be said in general that for intentional communities to play significant parts as pathfinders for better forms and spirit of social organizations they should be based on more inclusive and thoroughgoing study of all the elements which enter into satisfactory community life. As the view of life becomes more inclusive and better balanced there is a tendency for crusading zeal to grow less. Yet the survival and growth of any such undertaking depends as much on emotional commitment as on intellectual comprehension. Therefore zeal often holds the field as against broad insight and balanced judgment.

Nevertheless, in my opinion the future lies in just that broad, well-informed and well-balanced outlook, combined with strong drive of purpose and great commitment. Perhaps the world waits for just that union of qualities, and whoever helps to provide a setting where that general type of personality may have comradeship with its kind, and a social climate where children can grow up under the influence of such a way of life, may be performing a significant service, even though the size of operation may be very small.

Full, well-proportioned development does not imply uniformity. An individual can scarcely be said to have all-round, well-proportioned development unless he has become a master in some field.

It is the same with communities. A good community seeks not only balance and good proportion within itself, but it will seek to be an effective and valuable element within a larger society. It will seek to keep its own unique character, and to make its own unique contribution. In a group of adjacent communities the several units may each perform some service which helps the whole to meet varied needs. As a large number of individual communities and groups of communities develop their own unique characteristics and services in the process of becoming all-round social units, they will add to the richness and variety of the total national culture.

XVI

The Control and Discipline of Power in the Community of the Future

The taming, control and wholesome redirection of arbitrary power and ambition constitutes one of the greatest, if not the greatest practical problem of human society. In ancient times, when each community was an almost independent social and political unit, the prevailing folkways included effective methods for preventing the centralization of personal power. The widespread extent of these methods over nearly the whole world, and their great diversity, suggest that they were dealing with a major issue.

With the emergence of mass populations, with the coming of feudalism and empire, and with the growth of cities, the ancient small-community techniques and customs for the control and discipline of power broke down, and as yet have not been fully recovered. The history of empire for the past five thousand years is largely the story of uncontrolled or inadequately controlled power and ambition.

In the primitive community democratic government was one of the effective methods for keeping power within bounds. With its recent re-emergence democracy again becomes a powerful instrument to that end. However, personal and group ambition often is adaptive and resourceful. Men may observe the "rules of the game" in society, and may then use those very rules to take control and to extend selfish power. Some of the very mechanisms developed for the control and discipline of power are captured and used for extending and entrenching it. Among these is the democratic process of voting. Personal and group ambition have developed machine politics, in which persons with ambition for power may use the democratic process of voting to control public policy and public resources, and to shield economic or other exploiters, and even organized crime, from control. This is not the place for a discussion of the philosophy of ambition and power, except as they relate to the community of the future.

In America today the small community finds its normal life invaded by ambition and power from many directions. The political party machine tries to subordinate local government to machine politics. Voters are urged to vote the party ticket straight, down to local officials. In thousands of American small communities the state or county party committee tends to dominate the local party committee, and through it largely determines who the local government officials shall be and what policies shall prevail locally. By this method gambling and crime sometimes are sheltered and made sources of tribute, even in communities where a generally high standard of personal character prevails.

The community of the future in its local affairs must break free from such servitude to party and machine politics. It must have freedom to work out its own local policies and to choose its own officers. Some methods to that end, such as eliminating party designations in the listing of candidates, and adoption of the council-manager form of government, have proved helpful, though they are not cures for lack of civic interest and concern.

Centralized government also infringes upon the reasonable freedom of the community by absorbing vast financial resources through the taxing power, and then, in the administration of that power, taking away the normal and reasonable functions of the community. To some extent this may be inevitable, but the community of the future will be constantly on guard to protect itself from unnecessary reduction of its local autonomy. If the central government is the only effective agency for collecting revenues, it should return as large part of them as is feasible to the local community for its use according to its own design, though commonly under reasonable supervision to prevent abuse or local incompetence.

In the field of public education, with the half-conscious craving for more power on the part of state boards of education, bureaucratic ambition and educational megalomania are destroying the community structure of schools and are using very undue strategy, pressure and propaganda to carry school consolidation far beyond its desirable social limits. When the educational bureaucrat by inadvertence has expressed his real attitude he has said that parents and community are unfit for the guidance of school policy, and has held that the direction of the growth of children is a function of the state—that is, of the educational bureaucrat—and not of parent or community. Administrators also have approved and practiced strategic manipulation of state school funds to force their policies on communities.

Competing ideologies today fight strenuously, sometimes in the open, but more often in a quiet war of textbooks, for control of the child's mind, and in that process there is small regard for traditional culture. A few decades ago there was distributed in many of the public schools of my state a book promoted by the private utilities, presented for textbook use or collateral reading, the aim of which was to condition the mind of children against public ownership of power. At about the same time there was a widespread movement to condition the minds of school children, through "social science" textbooks, to a belief that our present social and economic system is obsolete and should be displaced by a planned semi-Marxian society. At the present time the United States Army is distributing textbooks through the schools which aim to develop in high school students the particular attitudes desired by the army in its training program. Such propaganda is presented in general before the age of reflective thinking. The community of the future will endeavor to recover and to maintain elementary education as a field of action for home and community, giving recognition to those near universals of human opinion which are generally recognized. Freedom in education will be a deliberate aim.

The relation of the state board of education to the local school system should be somewhat like the present relations between the state factory inspector and private industry. It should require maintenance of generally good human relations and should prevent negligence and exploitation. Otherwise the community should be free to devise and administer its own educational program. Such distribution of authority need not interfere with state or other agencies making available counsel and suggestions. Quite obviously, as boys and girls approach maturity they may grow beyond the capacity of the small, local community to serve them, and educational administration may need to be in larger social units, though not under state dictatorship.

In economic life also there is a tendency in many cases to reduce the local small community to servitude to the locally dominant industrial power. This subject is touched on in the chapter on the economics of the community of the future.

One of the oldest and most persistent forms of domination of the small community by arbitrary power has been in the field of religion. Repeatedly through the centuries in the Western world there have been efforts of small groups to achieve freedom in religion. These efforts have been met by the monolithic totalitarianism of the religious continuity of the Roman Empire. The Waldensians, a fine, strong, moral and self-respecting group, were hounded, massacred and persecuted by the church until they were reduced to the few who survived in the high mountains and along a national boundary line where they could cross back and forth to avoid pursuit. The Anabaptists of Central Europe, of which the Mennonites remain as descendants, had somewhat similar experience with both Luther and the Roman church. The Bogomils of eastern Europe, and the Albigenses of western Europe, were so completely eliminated by religious persecution and massacre that all we know about them is from the writings of their enemies. Yet even through these intentionally hostile accounts shines some of their great human quality. Seldom has man's inhumanity to man reached greater extremes than in such efforts to suppress religious freedom.

Fortunately today the cruder forms of coercion are not sustained in the relatively free atmosphere of our country, and we must go to South America to find physical violence still exercised. Yet in many American communities there is nearly complete absence of the democratic spirit and process in the field of religion. We are reminded of the earlier days of the "divine right of kings, " when any suggestion of political democracy was looked upon as irreverent and impious. The community of the future will seek freedom in its religious life as in other elements of living. To withhold self-direction in that field is to narrow the base of community life.

It is an almost universal human trait for the people of any culture or class or nation to idealize themselves, and to see grave faults in others. Men are very skillful in expunging from their own national or religious histories the pages of dishonor, and in seeing shameful traits only in aliens. Our country is no exception to that rule. In our relations with the American Indians our predominance of power was very great, and we could look at the enemy as a nuisance in the way of our manifest destiny, rather than as a menace to our existence.

America has omitted or expunged from her school histories the sordid truths concerning her exercise of power in relation to the Indians. Where the Indians were initially treated with honor and respect they nearly always responded with the same attitudes. Once betrayed, they "fought fire with fire." Except for the great difference in the scale of operations, there are few darker pages in the treatment of foreign or alien groups in the operations of Hitler or Stalin than some of those in our treatment of the American Indian. And this has been true in the history of our treatment of their religion as well as in the determination to stamp out the Indians' ancient custom of common ownership of land, and to "Americanize" them. That latter effort continues to the present.

Power is not something which bad men abuse, and which good men use to the glory of God. Irresistible power, such as that of the United States government against the Indians, is very liable to abuse by Americans and other saints. From the time of the writing of *A Century of Dishonor* and *Ramona* by Helen Hunt Jackson more than sixty years ago, to John Collier today, Americans have had a chance to be aware of the treatment of American Indians by their army and their government, and by persons wanting their land. There still remains opportunity for some persons to make a life work of restoring to these people a chance to live their own lives in their own communities, with their ancient "sacred" custom of communal ownership of their land. The subject is in the front of my mind because while writing this chapter I received a letter from two former students who are now making a study of some of these ancient communities, which emphasized their present status.

There are less obvious and less formal ways in which the small community, and American life as a whole, are brought under servitude to financial and social power. For instance, there is the matter of fashion in dress. Where can one find more abject servitude to coolly calculated ambition and self-interest? Economic interests from designers to manufacturers work out a style program and then undertake to impose it on the American public. And who dare defy it? In the community of the future it may come about that the people will be free from servitude to fashion, as in other ways. Would not America be a more interesting country if a thousand communities had each freely explored the possibilities of dress and had developed its own style? In recent years there is constantly increasing evidence of freedom, or at least variety of expression, in this field.

The community of the future must have the necessary freedom for exercise of its common functions. Otherwise the base of community life shrinks, and there is less opportunity for fellowship and participation.

Power and the Feeling of Crisis. One way in which power tries to control the public mind is by creating and maintaining a feeling of crisis. In a city where the relations of the city government to certain utilities were under serious question a feeling of crisis was developed over the claimed inadequacy of police protection. Since danger of physical harm touches people emotionally, it was possible in considerable degree to divert public attention from consideration of possible improper relations of the city government.

It has long been an axiom of "practical" politics that domestic unrest can often be averted by foreign war. When the nation's life is in danger is it not disloyal to pay attention to domestic troubles? During the first World War there was effort to bring as nearly as possible the whole attention of the nation to bear on the one issue of the national military effort. It was the "war to end war." Under such a crisis-of-all-the-ages was it not near disloyalty to be concerned with maintenance of public school standards? During succeeding years indoctrination of recruits by the West Point tradition included definitely pro-authoritarian and anti-democratic conditioning. (We are informed that the temper of that institution has now markedly changed for the better.) The plea was that under the threat of national disaster, against which the military was the major protection, political theory must give way before the demands of practical military competence. As a military man put it in the *Army and Navy Journal*, "Either our country is everything, or it is nothing."

When any element of life has attention out of proportion to the rest, there is danger. There are certain standards of integrity and honor on the part of individuals which a man ought not to surrender, even at the demand of his government. That was the principle back of the war crimes trials of Germans by the United States and its allies after the second World War. These trials gave acknowledgment to a principle that has long called for recognition—that all loyalties and authorities are relative. There are matters concerning which the individual cannot properly be asked to surrender his freedom or judgment to the community; there are issues on which neither the individual nor the community can properly be asked to surrender freedom or responsibility to the larger government or to other power.

One of the ways most commonly used to achieve voluntary subordination to existing power is by creating a sense of crisis, for in supreme crisis all other rules may give way. In fact, the excuse or justification for immoral or unethical action commonly is that a crisis exists, which requires that "practical" action be taken, inconsistent with ethical principles that otherwise would be recognized and observed. A good, well-rooted community tends to resist the cry of "crisis." Ability to keep the whole of life in perspective, and resistance to being carried away by any one or a few elements from a feeling of crisis, is a basic characteristic of a good community, and also a basic characteristic of morality. Development of such ability may be a major element in the taming and control of power.

XVII

Through the Dark Valley

We have expressed the conviction that the small face-to-face community is not a folkway which has had an interesting and useful past, though it has now been made obsolete by the march of civilization; but rather that, just as the habit of breathing air will continue to be necessary for our physical life, no matter what social or economic changes may occur, so the relationships of the small community will continue to be necessary for the survival of the basic cultural qualities of humanity. We have pictured the vigor and stubbornness with which the essence of community has survived many stresses and catastrophes. We have indicated how the essence of the community of old may be integrated with the values of modern technology and urban culture to create a form of social unit which would have the advantages of both old and new, and the serious disadvantages of neither.

Yet, all the while we are expressing ourselves in this way we have a deep foreboding that perhaps the recognition of the value of community has come too late. Perhaps the currents of life that are running against it are so strong that the pattern of community will be entirely washed away, leaving human society to exist, if at all, on another plane—of power, skillful design and external controls, on the basis of "enlightened selfishness" rather than of being motivated by a spirit of good will, brotherhood and mutual confidence.

There are many facts to support that foreboding. First, there is the general scale of organization of modern life. What long-run chance is there for a small nation? Hitler's program of absorbing the small adjoining nations was checked, not by those small nations, but by that colossus among nations, the United States. Russia has absorbed Latvia, Lithuania, Estonia, Poland, Czechoslovakia, Rumania, Hungary, Bulgaria, Albania, Outer Mongolia, and other free or semi-independent countries. Finland, Austria, Greece, and Iran probably exist as independent countries only because of America in the background. China is absorbing North Korea, northern Viet Nam, Tibet and other independent or semi-independent countries, and is checked, not by the other small countries, but by the United States and its allies. India annexed or absorbed—probably wisely—more than 200 native states, and had already treated as subjects or wards about 25,000,000 "aborigenes" who would have preferred independence. The United States in its expansion conquered and eliminated scores of small, native, independent sovereignties, often with the frontier slogan that "the only good Indian is a dead Indian."

We have pointed out that community cannot exist as a shell without functions. Within large nations there is a constant tendency to absorb local and community functions by national governments, leaving the small units with progressively fewer responsibilities. Social security has become chiefly a national responsibility. The national government subsidizes school lunches, allots crop limits to farmers, determines whether an industry must recognize a union, sets minimum wages and maximum hours of work, finances local home construction, pays the cost of purely local flood protection, and in a steadily increasing number of ways takes over activities which formerly rested in the community, or at the furthest in the state. What the national and state governments do affects the village and its citizens more than what their own council does.

A considerable part of these changes are necessary and beneficial. What they illustrate is not primarily the improper course of government, but the dilemma of the small community. We repeat, in the course of life there are many situations where there is not simply a right way and a wrong way, but where any course taken has seriously harmful effects. The problem then is to design the best possible course under the circumstances.

In education we see the same tendency to eliminate the functions of the small community, though here in many cases the changes are not desirable or necessary. It is characteristic of bureaucracy that it is hungry for power. State boards of education are no exceptions. In state after state educational authorities have gone far toward removing from the local community the determination of educational policy and program. Because education often was the chief common activity through which the community was conscious of itself, with the disappearance of the local community school through consolidation promoted by state authorities, the local consciousness of many communities has faded away.

Universal military training, a form of education, orients young men away from the democratic community spirit and its values, and from democratic method. It inculcates reliance on force and on arbitrary authority. In economics the trend is similarly marked. For many years we have been urging the feasibility and desirability of small industries located and owned in the community, and they have been demonstrated to be feasible. Yet the tide seems to be running against them. We have discussed this issue in the chapter on economic life.

Big business and centralized power, which tend to be inimical to community, seem compelled by the current of the time. What but big, centralized trade unions can face big, centralized business? What but big, centralized government can discipline both industry and labor? What chance has little industry with big industry and big labor unions? How get even a book circulated widely without the mass publicity of the big publisher? What chance for anything but bigness?

The development of technology, while in some ways favoring the small community, in other respects threatens its death. In former days what people knew most about were local, home-town affairs. Today they learn about what they see or hear over television or radio, in which the home community seldom is mentioned. The small town paper is disappearing or is having a continually more difficult time. The big city daily circulates through the small towns. We are losing our acquaintance with the home community.

These media change our society in ways unprecedented in all human existence. Until recently, no matter how the community was infringed on by authority and despotism, much of children's life was at home or in the immediate neighborhood, and seldom did an alien voice enter that domain. The chief exception was when alien authoritarian religion took authority over childhood. Today radio and television, with little regard for the culture of family or community, are often more intimate and familiar than the voices of parents. A considerable proportion of children spend more time with radio and television than in the presence of parents. This revolution is more fundamental than those wrought by most emperors and armies.

Two thirds of our people now are urban, with community experiences fading into the background. As we have previously stated, where agriculture formerly called for 85% of the manpower of our people, and thereby forced a distribution of the population, it now uses only 13%, and a few decades may reduce that to 10%. Therefore the small agricultural town is no longer the necessity it was formerly. The urban pattern is spreading, so that many small towns are no longer controlled by community attitudes, but are little cities, with urban, rather than small community values. The urban, rather than the community pattern comes to control. Add all these influences to the centuries-old inclination of the more ambitious and intelligent villagers to migrate to the city, and what chance is there for the survival of the small community?

To ignore such conditions and to "hope for the best" would be wishful thinking. If we are to contribute to the community and to what it stands for, our course should be taken in the light of all such unfavorable circumstances.

Community has not been a tender plant, subject to every wind that blows. It often has withstood extremely adverse circumstances. War, tyranny, famine, flood, pestilence, and other vicissitudes have beaten against it, impoverishing, diluting, adulterating, exploiting, enslaving, expelling and disrupting it; yet in many cases it has survived and in some degree has continued to preserve and to transmit the fundamental essence of the cultural inheritance.

The fate of democracy has been an example of the persistence of that tradition. The primitive community was democratic. That democracy did not die a natural death from old age. Since free community was an obstacle to power and despotism, with the growth of unrestrained power and empire it was suppressed by every possible means, until even interest in democracy was considered to be treason.

It is part of our theological heritage to think of "the survival of the fittest" as survival of the best—this on the principle that "God's in his heaven and all's well with the world."

Yet survival of the fittest means no more than survival of the
power to survive. In human affairs, as elsewhere in the world
of life, power may survive at the expense of that which would
make life worth living. It is the essence of ethics and religion
that we live so as to increase the prospect for the survival of
excellence, that is, of quality which makes life more worth
living for the whole of life, even at the expense of personal
interest.

The Spanish Inquisition so completely stamped out free
religion that it has scarcely reappeared in 400 years. That
cultural tradition having been definitely broken, what has halt-
ingly re-emerged in its place has been, not free religion, but
antireligion. But for American intervention, Hitler's Germany doubtless would have annexed democratic Denmark and
Norway.

What survives is not necessarily excellence, but power to
survive, and sometimes in case of human affairs that statement can be shortened to: what survives is power. About the
chief unfinished business of humanity is the control, discipline
and taming of power, so that "the survival of the fittest" will
be in fact the survival of excellence.

As to democracy, the degree of its suppression was not
evidence of its lack of value, but only of its lack of power
under the new conditions presented by the massing of population so that it was not possible for each person to know every
other person in his society. After many centuries of suppression of democracy, its opportunity has come again in various
parts of the world. As it emerges we see that it is not the
horrid thing which the long centuries of despotism had indoc-
trinated men to believe. It is well that the tradition of democracy was not completely broken, and thereby lost, though it
seemed to have been completely defeated except in a few use-
less corners or in the stubborn persistence of its spirit among
the peasantry. We mention the spirit of democracy as a case
in which for long periods its very small degree of power was
not a measure of excellence, and also as an instance where a
cultural inheritance persisted and survived for a very long
period against great odds.

A remarkable instance of the survival of the spirit of democracy and of community, with their qualities of human dig-

nity, is that of the American Indian. In a former publication we have quoted from John Collier's *Indians of the Americas*,[21] but the present theme justifies a repetition. He wrote:

> For years I believed that the long, remorseless course of events, the social destruction piled on biological destruction which the white man had wrought upon the Indians, must have killed, in most Indians, that most profound of their spiritual possessions. . . .
>
> The white conqueror, for reasons military, economic and religious, pronounced sentence of death on the Indian societies. Through century-long years of slavery, expropriation, physical decimation, and propaganda directed to the Indian against the Indian spirit, the conqueror worked hard to carry out the Indian's death sentence. . . .
>
> It was among the Plains Indians that the policy of annihilation of the societies and then of the individual Indian personality was carried to the farthest extreme. . . . Beginning about 1870, a leading aim of the United States was to destroy the Plains Indians' societies through destroying their religions; and it may be that the world has never witnessed a religious persecution so implacable and so variously implemented. . . . The assault against the tribal and inter-tribal religions was part of an all-out offensive against Indian land and society. . . . To kill the Indian traditions and to break the relationship of the generations, Indian children were seized at six years and were confined in "boarding schools" until past their adolescence. In vacation time they were indentured to whites as servants. In the schools the use of the native languages was forbidden; everything reminiscent of or relevant to Indian life was excluded; the children were forced to join whichever Christian church, through the favor of the Indian Bureau, had entrenched itself in the particular school.
>
> There was no method of destruction that was not used against them, and most of them coped with all the methods of destruction. Legal proscription, administrative proscription; military slaughter, enslavement, *encomienda*, forced labor, peonage; confiscation of nearly all lands, forced individualization of residual lands; forced dispersal, forced mass migration, forced religious conversions; religious persecutions which hunted down the social soul to its depths, and the propaganda of scorn; catastrophic depopulation, which mowed down the native leadership and the repositories of tradition; bribery of leadership, and the intrusion of quisling governments by the exploiting powers. . . .
>
> First, there was military assault, on slight pretexts or no pretext at all, and the government exploited tribal rivalries in order

that Indians should kill Indians. The limited and disciplinary war-customs of the Plains turned into total warfare, aimed at annihilation, with the United States Army as the driving power. The tribes were finally beaten, however, not through overwhelming numbers or superior armament (though these existed), but through starvation after the whites had destroyed the buffalo. . . .

Treaties and agreements were made, and in a few years unilaterally broken by the United States.... The buffalo was destroyed. That revelry of slaughter, which had no sportsmanship in it, was recognized as a war measure against the Indians and was deliberately encouraged.

Indian group life—Indian societies—outwore all the destructions. . . . They sustained the core and genius of their way of life. When so very, very late . . . some of the white man's societies lifted their sentences of death from these all but invisible Indian societies, the response was a rush of human energy, a creativity industrial, civic, esthetic. How swiftly, with what flashing brilliance, with what terrible joy, these long immured, suddenly reprieved little societies demonstrated the truth which our age has lost: that societies are living things, sources of the power and values of their members. . . .

The Indians and their societies disclose that social heritage is far more perduring than is commonly believed. On how small a life-base, on a diminished and starved life-base for how many generations, the motivations and expectations of a society, and its world-view and value systems and loyalties, can keep themselves alive; how these social possessions, which are of the soul, can endure, like the roots and seeds on the Mojave desert, through long ages, without one social rain; and how they rush, like these roots and seeds, into surprising and wonderful blossom when the social rain does come at last. . . . This capacity for perdurance is one of the truths on which the hope of our world rests. . . . The sunken stream can flow again, the ravaged desert can bloom, the great past is not killed. (Quotations out of sequence, but not out of meaning; italics added.)

The fact that the spirit and structure of numerous Indian communities survived the drive to extinguish them—which might be called "the great American inquisition"—testifies to the vitality of the community spirit. But that such survival was by no means inevitable is indicated by the fact that many fine native cultures were entirely exterminated.

Does it seem immoderate to refer to such extreme cases as those of the American Indian, and of the survival of democracy in a hostile world, to justify our hope that the spirit of community is strong enough to survive the assaults being made upon it, and the more concentrated attacks which may be made in the future ? The types of attack which must be resisted are quite different, yet perhaps no less menacing. It may be that for a long time to come the face-to-face community will be on the defensive, holding one mountain fortress or one forgotten valley after another, until the day comes when its full value and full significance will be generally recognized. Some villages will work out their own independent programs, enduring for the time such encroachments as they cannot avoid. Some community school systems will work out their programs without dictation from above, again making concessions where they cannot be avoided, but not losing the aim. Many small businesses, if only in the interstices of our economic society, will work out the spirit of community in their structures and operation, notwithstanding the pressures of big business, big unions and big government. Some democratic, free, religious fellowships will keep the faith against the current of the times. Sometimes all these elements will be associated in one locality. For perhaps a long time, those who pioneer for community will be minorities; but it is minorities with sound direction and purpose which make history.

Yet the time may not be very long. Humanity is in flux. New patterns will emerge. If some of those are inherently sound their support may grow more rapidly than we expect. There are qualities in man which crave freedom, dignity, good will, absence of suspicion and strategy. Men will tend to congregate where those are in evidence or to support them where they appear.

But there is quite another approach to community survival and increase. It is not in conflict with that we have just stated, but parallel to it and in harmony with it. The essence of community is fullness and fineness of life, in which the motives men live by are those which have our deepest respect, and in which the physical and social setting are most favourable to enduring values. Thus community is made up of many elements. While the aim is to achieve them all in good proportion, yet opportunities most often come, not to fulfill an entire pattern, but to perfect some of its elements. The more we see our pattern as a whole, the more we will recognize the various elements of opportunity as they appear.

We knew a small town schoolteacher many years ago who observed that one of her pupils had no associations which provided the friendship, sympathy and encouragement which are characteristics of a true small community, and was "going wrong." She supplied the friendship and belief in him which he needed. As it happened he was for a generation later the most influential figure in the community, and the pattern of life she disclosed to him became his own. Opportunities for furthering community come to every person. It may be that the local school system needs friendly help. Perhaps an employer of a small force develops in his employees and in himself the industrial attitudes which would characterize a good community. To do that on even a small scale may require a revolution in the employer's attitude toward life and industry. In achieving such a change in himself and in his undertaking a man may make a greater contribution than though he were in a very conspicuous public position. Perhaps our opportunities may seem to be smaller, yet they will not be absent.

The texture of community is made up of many threads of living. As many individuals make their own parts consistent with the character of a good community, a social climate will emerge which in the long run is what constitutes community, and what constitutes good human relations. No matter how adverse one's own situation may be, he will have opportunity in some form to help to create the community of the future. And seldom is any piece of work well done but that it opens the way to other opportunity. Even defeat, when it comes from standing firm for what is most suitable but unpopular, commonly leads to further opportunity. So the building of the new community will consist of achieving of many elements.

We believe it is well to have pointed out the very heavy odds which the spirit of community must face in the years to come. To expect an easy course might lead to a feeling of defeat and frustration. A man in a boat was being swept down a coastal estuary and out to sea by the outgoing tide. Though he rowed as hard as he could, he steadily lost position. He was not discouraged, for he knew that tides do not last forever. By reducing the rate of his losing ground he would be in better position when the tide should come in.

Recent anthropologists hold that the time which has elapsed since our ancestors branched off from all other species of primates and took the distinct path to humanity, is in the order of 20,000,000 years. During probably the whole of that period our ancestors were small community creatures, and achieved adjustment to small community life, vestiges of which have come down to us in such expressions as the Sermon on the Mount and similar attitudes in other parts of the world. Then, perhaps ten thousand years ago, a revolution took place in human affairs which resulted in nations, armies, cities, and despotisms. Evidently our species is in transition to another and more inclusive harmony. Because the present human turmoil has lasted through the course of human history, say 6000 years, we are inclined to think of it as a permanent condition of humanity. However, if we take the period during which our line has been distinct from any other—say 20,000,000 years —as equal to 24 hours, then a period of twice the length of human history would be less than a minute long on that scale.

Even if most of those conditions which we have referred to as interfering with the arrival of the community of the future should last for centuries, they still would represent a transient period of transition—that is, if the slowly won valuable elements of the cultural inheritance are not lost. Should they be wholly lost, then the course of human life might take a distinctly different direction, based on enlightened selfishness and strategy and power, rather than on good will and mutual confidence. To insure that the spirit of community is not lost is the adventure on which we are engaged.

REFERENCES

1. *The Christian Century*, LXXIII, No. 32 (August 8, 1956).
2. *Coronet* magazine, Vol. 36, No. 6, p. 68.
3. George Peter Murdock, *Social Structure* (New York, Macmillan Company, 1949), pp. 79–80.
4. *Holy Bible*, Revised Standard Version: *Amos*, 2:6, 5:7; *Isaiah*, 5:8; 29:15-16; 59:8; 32:7-8, 14, 16-17; 33:15-16.
5. Machiavelli, *The Prince* (in part from translation of N. H.Thomson in the *Harvard Classics;* in part from *The Living Thoughts of Machiavelli*, "presented by" Count Carlo Sforza (New York, Longmans, Green and Company, 1940).
6. Vilhjalmur Stefansson, in *I Believe* (Clifton Fadiman, ed.; New York, Simon and Schuster, 1939), pp. 266-7, 269, 271, 275.
7. *Kautilya's Arthasastra*, translated by R. Shamasastry (Mysore, India; the Wesleyan Mission Press, 1929).
8. *Holy Bible*, Revised Standard Version, *I Corinthians* 13.
9. Bliss Perry, *And Gladly Teach* (Boston, Houghton Mifflin, 1935).
10. George H. Palmer, *The Autobiography of a Philosopher* (Boston, Houghton Mifflin, 1930).
11. Stephen Decatur, Toast, Norfolk, Virginia, April, 1816.
12. George C. Homans, *The Human Group* (New York, Harcourt, Brace and Company, 1950), pp. 318, 22, 455-6, 277, 369.
13. *Encyclopedia Britannica*, article on Kekule.
14. Poincare, *Science and Method* (Science Press, 1913), *Mathematical Discovery* and *Science and Hypothesis* (Walter Scott Publishing Company, England, 1914); Jacques Hadamard, *The Psychology of Invention in the Mathematical Field* (Princeton University Press, 1945); J. W. N. Sullivan, *The Limitations of Science* (New York, New American Library, 1949; Viking Press, 1933).
15. Sir George Aston, article on Egypt in *Britannica*, 14th edition.
16. H. Fielding Hall, *The Soul of a People* (London, Macmillan, 1908); more extensively quoted in *The Heritage of Community*, published by Community Service, Inc., 1955.
17. Sorokin *et al.*, *A Systematic Source Book in Rural Sociology* (University of Minnesota Press, 1932).
18. Griscom Morgan, in *Bottom-Up Democracy*, Community Service, Inc., 1955).
19. Don J. Bogue, *Structure of the Metropolitan Community* (Ann Arbor, University of Michigan, 1950).
20. W. R. Alger, *The Genius of Solitude* (Boston, 1867).
21. John Collier, *Indians of the Americas: The Long Hope* (New York, New American Library, 1948), pp. 11, 15, 132-4, 183, 133, 183, 15-16, 171.

· INDEX

(The topical Table of Contents effectively supplements this index.)

Damascus: changing culture of, 43
Dayton, Ohio: duration of industries in,
51
Decatur, Stephen, military figure: "my
country, right or wrong," 38
Declaration of Independence: signers
mostly rural, 49
Democracy, ancient: did not die natural
death, 155

Economics, community: variety necessary, 99; autonomy in, 115-118
—industrial standards suggested: freedom, 102; reasonableness, 103; a
fair profit, 103-107; business must
pay, 107; open records, 108; business competence, 108; continuity,
108; obligations to employees, 109;
steady operation, 110; responsibility, 110; elimination of waste, 111;
reconciliation of controversies,
112; restraint on personal ambition,
112; control of size, 112; desirable
incentives, 113; right relation to
other interests, 113
Education: vitalizes community, 58;
bureaucratic power in, 154
Egypt: celibacy in, 24; decadence of, 45
Either-or dogma, 5
Ellis, Havelock, English writer: on
urban population, 50
Emerson, Ralph Waldo: on urban de-
generacy, 50
Emotional quality: important, 37
Eskimos: individual yet social, 5, 10,
23, 31, 32
Exceptional persons: community will
prepare for, 85
Exchange credits, 117

Family: changing needs of, with age,
87-88; and community, universal
social forms, 20
Farms: decline of population on, 155
Fellah, Egyptian: dependability of, 45
Finland: persistence of quality in, 47;
love of nature in, 82
Franklin, Benjamin: quoted, 57
Friends, Society of: decision by con-
sensus in, 94

Galton, Francis, English writer: on
urban population, 50
Gandhi, Mahatma: ideas on Basic Edu-
cation, 128
Gemeinschaft and gesellschaft, 4
Gordon relief expedition, 45
Government, local: criteria for, 96
Greeks: wide travelers, 61

Hall, H. Fielding, writer: on Burmese
character, 46
Holmes, O. W., 7, 157
Homans, George C., sociologist, 42;
on intellectuals, 38, 57
Home: changing needs of, 87-88
Home rule: vs. equal rights, 91, 92
Hopi Indian families: child develop-
ment in, 127
Hutterites: culture patterns of, 10;
communities, 143

Ibn Khaldun, Arab scholar: on city
decadence, 50
Ideologies, competing, 147
Indians, American; bad treatment of,
149; persistence of culture of, 157;
Miami, migrations of, 76
Industrial towns, 74
Industries: advantages of small-scale,
101; survival rate of, 51
Industry: excessive size of, 103
Inquisition, Spanish, 156
Interrelation: of communities, essen-
tial, 64, 65
Isaiah: quoted, 30, 31

Jackson, Helen Hunt, novelist: books
on Indians, 149

Kalevala: Finnish classic, 82
Kautilya: "Institution of Spies," 28,
32, 33
Kekule, Friedrich, chemist: discov-
ery of "benzene ring," 40
Kettering, Charles F., 124
Kibbutzim, Palestine communities, 143
Kingsley, Charles, English author, 24

Land reclamation: cooperation in, 65
Landlords: no soil fertility under, 44

Language: origin and evolution of, 8, 9, 18
Levels of organization, 27
Le Play, Frederic, French sociologist, 3
Library: should serve exceptional persons, 84
Love: as emotion and as purpose, 37; as nepotism, 37; as patriotism, 37, 38; its function in community, 36; undisciplined, may be harmful, 37

Machiavelli, N., 28, 29, 32
Maine, Henry Sumner, English writer, 3
Marriages: intercommunity, common, 61
Marx, Karl: on child labor, 129
Merck, Johann Heinrich: friend of Goethe, 1
Migration: effect on community of individual, 61
Mormon communities, 143
Murdock, George P., anthropologist, 20

Natural beauty: diversity of, 83
Nature conditions: changes in, 85
New Mexico: ancient irrigation in, 65

Ortega y Gasset, Jose, writer, 57
Ohio Conservancy Act: cooperative action under, 65

Palmer, George Herbert, philosopher, 36
Peasantry: persistence of quality in, 47
Perry, Bliss, educator, 36
Pessimism, scientific, 38, 39
Physical plant: not necessarily permanent, 75
Planned communities, 74
Poincare, J. H., on creative thinking, 40
Progressive Education Association, 125, 126, 128
Prosperity: and cultural decline, 45; man not acclimated to, 86
Public interest: how determined, 69

Quakers: divine guidance or creative thinking among, 39; decision by consensus among, 94

Regional service associations, 66
Revelation: associated with cultural tradition, 40
Revenge: "wild justice," 17
Rome: decay of, 43, 45
Rousseau, Jean Jacques: totalitarian philosophy of, 68, 69; inverted "total depravity" doctrine, 142
Russia: absorption of small nations by, 153

Sanderson, Dwight, American sociologist, 3
Santa Maria island: village on, 98, 99
Saturnalia, 24
School system, American: brought from Germany, 126; rigidity of, 127
Scythians, 42
Sex customs: have pragmatic origin, 17
Simeon Stylites, columnist, 1
Sintra (Portugal): beauty of, 83
Small business: may survive in interstices of society, 159
Small industry: tide runs against it, 154
Social controls: three kinds, 14, 38; are there infallible, 39
"Social eugenics," 63, 64
Social tradition: as social control, 15, 16, 38; in animals, 17
Soil fertility: vs. landlordism, 44
Solitude: value of, 79, 80, 81
Species: extinction of, 53
Speech: origin of, 8; evolution of, 9, 18, 21
Spies, "Institution of," 32, 33
Split personality of society, 53; can be cured, 56
Stefansson, Vilhjalmur, explorer, author: on Eskimos, 31, 32
Sugar: taste for may mislead, 16
Survival vs. excellence, 156
Swiss: respect for exceptional quality, 84

Technical possibilities for community, 87
Technology: effect on community, 55
Tennyson, Alfred, poet, 53
Teutonic League: created communities, 139